W H AUDEN

by Stephen Wade

GREENWICH EXCHANGE
LONDON

for Paul

Other books by Stephen Wade include:

Isherwood, (1991)

More on the Word Hoard, (1993)
- Essays on Seamus Heaney

The Imagination in Transit, (1996)
- The fiction of Philip Roth

Churwell Poems, (1987)

Greenwich Exchange

First published in Great Britain in 1997

W H Auden © Stephen Wade, 1997
All rights reserved

Printed and bound by Priory Press, Holywood, N. Ireland.

ISBN 1-871551-36-6

CONTENTS

CHRONOLOGY

1907   Wystan Hugh Auden born in York. The family then moves to Birmingham in 1908.

1915-20   Attends St. Edmund's preparatory school. His friendship with Christopher Isherwood begins.

1920-25   At Gresham's School in Holt. His first poem is published in 1924.

1925-8   Goes to Christ Church College, Oxford. *Poems* collection is printed privately by Stephen Spender.
May, 1926 General Strike
1927 BBC established
1928 Vote is given to women on equal terms with men.

1928-9   Auden is in Berlin. He meets John Layard, whose psychological ideas influence Auden's thought. Layard attempts suicide. "He wanted me to finish him off" was Auden's comment.
1929 A Labour government formed under Ramsay Macdonald.

1930-35   Auden starts teaching at Larchfield Academy in Helensburgh, Scotland, and then at the Downs School, Colwall, Malvern. In 1933, he has a revelatory experience while watching people on the lawn of the school one evening.
Poems   1930
The Orators   1932
He is influenced by D. H. Lawrence's book, *Fantasia of the Unconscious*. He also begins working on plays with Isherwood.
1932 Nazis become the largest party in the Reichstag.
1933 Hitler becomes Chancellor.

1935   Writes *The Dog Beneath the Skin* with Isherwood. Works for six months with the GPO Film Unit, working on the documentary, *Coal Face* with the composer, Benjamin Britten; then on *Night Mail*.
Edits an anthology, *The Poet's Tongue*, with John Garrett.

1936	Trip to Iceland with Louis MacNeice. They write the travel book, *Letters from Iceland*, published in 1937. Also writes *The Ascent of F6* with Isherwood. In Iceland, he sees the depths of man's potential for senseless cruelty in the slaughter of whales at Talknafjordur. *Look, Stranger!* published. Abdication of Edward VIII. Spanish Civil War begins.
1937	Goes to Spain during the Civil War, under the auspices of the Spanish Medical Aid Committee, writing a report for the *New Statesman*. Writes his poetic commentary on events in the poem *Spain 1937*. Meets Charles Williams, poet and religious writer. Chamberlain succeeds Baldwin as Prime Minister.
1938	Commissioned to write on the Chinese-Japanese War in Manchuria. This is written with Isherwood under the title, *Journey to a War*. Also writes *On the Frontier* with Isherwood. Hitler annexes Austria.
1939	Auden and Isherwood move to the United States. They are ridiculed in Evelyn Waugh's *Put Out More Flags* as Parsnip and Pimpernel. Auden meets Chester Kallman, with whom he forms a deep and lasting relationship. 'We're something more exciting than just good friends'. Hitler invades Poland. Second World War begins.
1940	*Another Time* published. He is influenced by the philosopher and religious thinker, Søren Kierkegaard. He reverts to Christianity. Churchill becomes Prime Minister. Dunkirk evacuation of B. E. F. troops.
1941	Teaches at Olivet College, University of Michigan. Works on an opera, *Paul Bunyan*, with Benjamin Britten. *The Double Man* (*New Year Letter* in England). Hitler invades Russia. Atlantic Charter signed.
1942	Teaches at Swarthmore College, Pennsylvania, and at Brywn Mawr. He is rejected by the military draft board.

1944	*For the Time Being* published.
	Allied invasion of Normandy.
1945	Visits Europe, sees his father in the Lake District. April: recruited to the Morale Division of the U.S. Strategic Bombing Survey in Germany.
	Atomic bombs dropped on Japan.
	Labour government with Atlee.
1946-7	Teaches at Bennington and Barnard colleges. Buys a 'retreat' in Long Island.
	The Age of Anxiety published.
	edits the Yale series of Younger Poets 1947-57
	Nuremburg war trials.
1948	Writes moral parables: in opera libretti, working with Kallman.
	Awarded Pulitzer Prize for *The Age of Anxiety*.
	Gandhi assassinated. Russians blockade Berlin. Allied air lift.
	1949 North Atlantic Treaty
1950	*Collected Shorter Poems* published. *The Enchafed Flood.*
	Edits *Poets of the English Language* with N. H. Pearson.
	Korean War begins.
1951	Auden and Kallman write the libretto for Stravinky's *The Rake's Progress*
	Nones published. With Jacques Barzun, he manages the Readers' Subscription Book Club.
	Conservative government under Churchill returned.
1952	Does his first important lecture tour of the United States.
	Accession of Elizabeth II. Korean War ends.
1954	Awarded the Bollinger Prize. Elected to the American Academy of Arts and Letters.
	U. S. hydrogen bomb tested at Bikini Atoll.
1955-6	*The Shield of Achilles* published. Receives National Book Award for 1956.
	Suez crisis. Russian tanks put down Hungarian uprising.
1956-61	Elected Professor of Poetry at Oxford. Gives inaugural lecture, 'Making, Knowing and Judging' (published in *The Dyer's Hand*).
	Awarded the Feltrinelli Foundation prize of $33,000. Leaves Ischia with Kallman and buys a house at Kirchstetten in Austria.

1958	*Selected Poetry* published.
	European Common Market founded. CND launched.
1960	*Homage to Clio* published. *Lady Chatterley* trial.
1961-3	*The Dyer's Hand* (critical essays) 'a kind of literary autobiography'.
	With Kallman, writes a libretto for Henze's *The Bassarids*.
	Becomes interested in the life and writings of Goethe. With Elizabeth Mayer, translates Goethe's *Italian Journey*. The desertion of Kallman affects him deeply.
	Kennedy assassinated.
1964	Receives an honorary degree from Swarthmore College.
1965-6	In Berlin. His health deteriorates. Also, he is affected by T. S. Eliot's final illness.
1967	Homosexual acts between consenting adults legalised in Great Britain.
1966-9	Writes increasingly political poems. Takes a deeper interest in the machinations of power. *About the House 1966*.
	Attends the first Poetry International in London. (1967)
	In 1968 Kallman's friend, Boras, is killed in a road accident.
	1966 U. S moon landing. *Epistle to a Godson* 1969
1970	*A Certain World*, Auden's 'commonplace book' published.
1972	Settles in Oxford.
1973	*Forewords and Afterwords*, collected and edited by Edward Mendelson, published. Sept. 28. Dies in his sleep.

INTRODUCTION

'The test of a poet is the frequency and diversity of the occasions on which we remember his poetry.'   *The Poet's Tongue*

'. . . . . . since psychological truth depends so largely on context, poetry, the parabolic approach, is the only adequate medium for psychology.'   *The Poet's Tongue*

Auden is a poet whose writings are full of complexities and contradictions. His range of narrative tones and attitudes can sometimes seem like the stance of a conscious sage, sometimes like a playful farceur. His poems may take allegorical depth or bite sarcastically into his dislikes; they may convey the certainty of an aphorism or the doubts and dilemmas of a mind troubled by what Thomas Hardy called 'the ache of modernism'. What is certain, though, is his relevance both to today and to the continuing debates over the puzzle of what defines and characterises the human experience and state of being.

A cursory survey of his writing would most likely note the emergence of the quintessential social commentator of the 'Thirties, through the period of explaining love and religious experience, to the questionings of art and power of the later years. How does one define the qualities of a writer who has so many different literary influences behind him and broad intellectual interests, was Professor of Poetry at Oxford, lived in Berlin during the rise of Hitler, experienced extremes of human suffering, yet who could play the fool, be whimsical, boyish and outstandingly eccentric and perverse?

Some aspects of his achievement cannot be argued with; he has remained popular, in print and widely read. His most accessible lyrics have been given the status of 'set texts' for academic study since the sixties, and the use of his poetry in popular films (e. g. *Four Weddings and a Funeral*) has boosted sales of the two selections from his work recently reissued by Faber. With the popularity goes a stunningly wide

1

repertoire: his oeuvre covers dramatic verse, formal experiments, 'light' verse, opera libretti, long narrative poetry, essays and criticism.

Yet, there is a certain sententiousness, a tendency to pronounce, and perhaps also a cryptic element which asks us to decode much of the fabric of many of the poems even when there is no real substance there: particularly when he wants to encompass a whole range of issues or give a sweeping generalisation based solely on a feeling or an intuition. Too often, one feels, there is no real occasion for a poem: simply a development of a good line. Indeed, one of his attempts at defining poetry does so by calling it an intuitive glance built into a structure. This is the unapproachable side to Auden's work, and it continues to present problems to readers coming to his work for the first time. The difficulty lies in the syntax and the predominance of abstract diction.

He also made consistently important and serious pronouncements about the nature of poetry and of art in general, that should be taken equally seriously by anyone interested in how modern poetry reached its present status. Auden could apply philosophy or Freudian analysis to literature or speak in the way that Wordsworth wanted poetry to enter our everyday discourse: using 'the language of common men'. The universal appeal of Auden's shorter poems is explained by his ease with the contemporary idiom he displayed, despite Isherwood's claim that Auden pieced together stray lines from notebooks into cryptic lyrics, in *The Waste Land* vein. There appears to be some substance in this, but it doesn't explain all. It does not offer any enlightenment regarding the way that a multitude of influences filter through a lyric without pollution - in the early poetry, if not in the later.

Is there a 'typical' Auden poem? For the general reader it is characterised by three outstanding features: (a) a hauntingly dream-like 'inner landscape' for the setting; (b) a melancholy, wise voice which gives elegiac witness to a human presence in the poem and (c) a mix of lyrical celebration with brutal honesty about our emotional make-up. An Auden lyric is rarely an easy read. He asks the reader to cope with complex syntax and with a refined sensibility - often too self-indulgent to keep our sense of coherence in what we read. Perhaps 'Song' written in 1938, exemplifies these. The third stanza, spoken by the narrator from 'Bristol Street' in a surreal setting, gives us the hyperbole of the lovers' vows almost to the level of a Dali image:

'I'll love you dear. I'll love you
Till China and Africa meet
And the river jumps over the mountain
And the salmon sing in the street.'

The poem goes on to give a Blakean commentary on the modern condition of loving within the alienated city, delving into the 'new' patterns of relationships forced on twentieth century people after wars and revolution, anticipating further upheaval on the eve of the Second World War. Yet, despite all this, 'Life remains a blessing/ Although you cannot bless'.

The lyric sharpens appreciation of that helplessness and distance from 'real' relationships that so many poets since T. S. Eliot's *The Waste Land* (1922) have explored, but Auden stamps an undeniable originality on this theme.

The originality, the quirky eccentricity so closely monitored in the available biographies, is of central importance in understanding Auden the poet. His homosexuality, about which, despite protestations to the contrary, he felt guilty, his Christianity and his interest in Existential philosophy always catch the reader's attention. The reader is invited to reflect on himself, but there are always strands of entertainment, as in the witty *Letter to Lord Byron* written in 1936, where Auden gives us shreds of autobiography in playful mood:

'Our old cook Ada surely knew her stuff;
My elder brothers did not treat me rough;
We lived in Solihull, a village then;
Those at the gasworks were my favourite men.'

There have been dissenting voices of course. At worst, this could be seen as doggerel; at best, more a poem of sheer ingenuity. Many critics noted a decline in powers and achievement after *Homage to Clio* (1060). Philip Larkin, for instance, said, 'Auden has not, in fact, gone in the direction one hoped. . . he has recovered a dialect. . . it is all too often an extraordinarily jarring one.' Even Richard Hoggart, an admirer, calls his later work 'uneven'.

The problem lies in his often sententious expression that has lost admirers and created negative responses. Some of this dislike may have its roots in something peculiarly English and quite insular, inward-looking. Auden's mind and attitudes expressed something European rather than an idiom based securely on the tradition of that 'Englishness' associated mostly with the Georgian period epitomised by Edward Thomas, Walter de la Mare and others who celebrated a pastoral way of life and the neo-Wordsworthian rurality they wanted to see. There is an influence from Hardy detectable in Auden's work, and there is a strong sense of place and landscape in his poetry, but there is an alien vein too, an offshore perspective, the voice of a traveller, a visitor.

This springs from his wide reading and travel in his formative years, and also the alienation and detachment he felt due to his homosexuality. The vast range of writers discussed in his final volume, *Forewords and Afterwords* includes essays on Augustine and Housman, Lewis Carroll and Edgar Allan Poe. His profound interest in the mind and art of Goethe in his later years is indicative of his Pan-European sensibility. Goethe, the man who was an amateur scientist as well as a poet and dramatist, is understandably interesting to Auden who always saw the world with a panoramic vision, whether topographically or in dream-analysis.

George Orwell, in his long essay *Inside the Whale* (1940), made a passionate statement about the difficulties many readers have with Auden the 'Thirties writer and he labels Auden as one of a group characterised as having a 'serious purpose' contrasted with those who entertain and are not perhaps, in our terms, politically correct. Orwell criticises the poem 'Spain' and says, 'Mr. Auden's brand of amoralism is only possible if you are the kind of person who is always somewhere else when the trigger is pulled.' Orwell is arguing that Auden's cosmopolitan, detached stance is one element that excludes him from the 'Englishness' of the Georgian era which Orwell summarised earlier

4

in his essay. The Modernist in Auden is the artist who looks with a distant view, cold and scientific at times in his lyric voice when he tries to give us political satire or a commentary on events. One reason may be that he did not allow for the 'hearty' version of beefy Englishness exemplified in Forster's Wilcoxes to have any place in his ideal landscape.

What needs to be explored is the status of Auden as an influential poet whose work has elements of style derivative of the Hardy-Georgian period, yet also has the substance of the European poet, with a more open-ended view of the historical process and the exercise of state power. Auden never loses the faith that, as in Russia, the writer and intellectual is important, and speaks to all his or her contemporaries. As Jean-Paul Sartre said, 'We have a strange tradition in France - the artist is also a citizen'. Auden would have, one feels, included that in his credo; part of his search for the nature of love, which is also to be a focus of the present study - and he had plenty to say about being a 'citizen'.

Andrew Marvell's famous poem, 'The Definition of Love' written in the seventeenth century, is a succinct expression of many of Auden's concerns. The conclusion of Marvell's poem is:

'Therefore the love which us doth bind,
but Fate so enviously debarrs,
Is the conjunction of the Mind,
And opposition of the stars.'

Auden similarly examines the paradoxes in that bundle of feelings we refer to as 'love' and that word is probably the most often repeated word in his poetry.

As a Christian, he was well read in the importance of the distinction between that wider love for humanity, *agape,* (in Greek thought) and erotic love. His love poems are often about 'Fate' and also the willpower and sense of belonging that we pin on the word love, and in Auden's case, his interest was often a post-Freudian one, in the sense that he absorbed the simplistic methods of dream-analysis that any layman can extract from one key chapter in Freud's *The Interpretation of Dreams.*

He built much of his imaginative preoccupations on that central line of thought.

Finally, any introductory study of Auden has to relate his concerns for morality and art to his poetry. Here, my approach will be to look at some representative poems in depth. The difficulty lies in Auden's didacticism. If there is a central fatal flaw in Auden's basic attitude to poetry, it is to do with its social function. That is, perhaps his claims were too large. Even admirers of his work must recognise that the claims his work makes may be too great to be sustainable.

I A POET'S LIFE

Schooling and Oxford 1907-28

Wystan Hugh Auden was born in York on 21 February, 1907. His father, George, moved the family to Birmingham the following year, as he was to be a school medical officer in that city. Auden's parents had married in 1899. Auden had two brothers, of whom John was to be very close, and also quite similar to Wystan in character and interests.

Dr. Auden was a man with a wide range of interests in addition to medicine, in particular psychology and archaeology. The family had Icelandic origins. Wystan took up many of his father's interests, including topography, mining and a love of mountainous regions.

It was a religious household, but he reacted against religion as a young man, only to return to it in later life. His mother was quite clearly a profound influence on the whole family, and Auden's early work (up to the late 'Thirties particularly) contains several themes and metaphors relating to the image and meaning of the 'mother' in our formation of the sense of self.

In 1915 he was sent to St. Edmund's school in Hindhead, Surrey (with brother John) and it was then that he first met Christopher Isherwood, the novelist, who became one of his closest friends throughout life. During the time here and subsequently at Gresham's School in Holt, Norfolk from 1920, his interests and enthusiasms were very broad and eclectic, which were to become life-long traits. He particularly enjoyed science as well as poetry. It was here that he distanced himself from his earlier religious beliefs.

It was also at Holt that Auden established the firm conviction that he was to be a poet. This is documented as having been voiced during a walk with another new friend, Rupert Medley, in 1922. Early influences on his conception of what constituted poetry are most certainly Wordsworth, Hardy and Housman. Housman was particularly important, as the stoical-romantic and homo-erotic strain of *A Shropshire Lad*, such a deep influence on the generation who wrote

'Georgian' poetry and who fought in the Great War, and on these men's sons, is detectable in most of Auden's rhythms and cadences in the juvenilia and even in later poems. It is in the formative years of a poet, perhaps, that certain persistent inner rhythms and patterns of line and imagery find a niche. The Georgian mixture of worship, love of place and inner doubts find significant positions in Auden's mental landscape.

Unusually in the study of poetry, the case of Auden shows just how profoundly early influences may persist. Indeed, the case against Auden is that he never matured fully as a poet. The Auden generation took an interest in the experience of school, turning the 'first age' of life into a metaphor for what we would now call interpersonal relationships and sexual politics. School, whether in Orwell's memoirs, or in Betjeman's verse, played a central role in the formation of the literary preoccupations of thirties writers. For Auden, it was not only a shaping experience, but also sustenance for the poet's art.

Auden's idea of poetry as a vocation, acknowledged so early, is perhaps inexplicable in any easily-definable way; all that can be said from a distance over time and from a climate in which poetry is seen more as a hobby than a profession, is that the process is intuitive. Graves also held the view that poetry was his 'vocation'. Auden's belief that poetry offers no more than 'an intuitive glance' hints at the notion that poetry is a difficult art, with an apprenticeship and a range of skills to be mastered: the poet is a 'maker' in the classical tradition of the *vates*, a craftsman.

The early poetry is interesting in that he expressed a preference for places over people. In the pieces of autobiography quoted by Richard Davenport-Hines, for instance, there are comments such as:

'Country on a fine day always makes one feel, Why do I bother
with people? They are insignificant.'

The first landscapes were littered with references to his reading, his boyish enthusiasms, and his expression of aesthetic distancing from the world of middle-class order. But he did realise that both reading and writing poetry needed 'a special mental effort' and that there was a part played by the reader that was *active*. Auden had a resolution far from fully-formed, but undoubtedly very serious. The art of poetry was a way of assembling diverse mental thought processes, and one quality Auden always had was a tireless search for novelty in ideas as well as in life.

He was ready for Oxford, but what could Oxford offer such a headstrong individualist? Before going to university, he had acquired a great deal of self-belief, praise from others and a wide circle of friends. His academic preparation resembled that of many poets and writers before him - largely a frame of mind that read fitfully and without a scheme or clear sense of direction. He had a firm sense of what he liked and did not like, but had he acquired an objective sense? The story at Oxford was to be yet another example of the academic sustenance being only partially successful as a diet for a creative temperament. It seems that over-confidence was a flaw, also - not uncommon in poets and artists with a sense of vocation.

Oxford 1925-28

Auden went to Christ Church in 1925. Here he met Isherwood again, and fell deeply in love with a student, Bill McElwee. Stephen Spender was also in his circle of friends, and he was to be a close friend for life. Although Auden eventually took only a third-class degree, despite having the scholarly Chaucerian Nevill Coghill as his tutor, exciting experiences which affected his poetic stance and his intellectual position happened in the undergraduate years. He read, along with hundreds of other artistic, sensitive English literature students, T. S. Eliot's journal *The Criterion* and more particularly, he read *The Waste Land* in the spring of 1926.

Eliot's poem was so innovative and startling in form and in stylistic effects that it opened out immense possibilities, paradoxically, for the poetry of both social commentary and self-expression. The idea of the self in the modern world of dissociated sensibility naturally appealed to the Auden generation. By the late 'Twenties, it seemed possible that poetry could be a medium for expressing both personal alienation and political commitment.

In Auden's case, this was given more substance by his developing interest in psychoanalysis. His notions of art and of the aesthetic sense within everyday consciousness were closely linked to the suppressed significance of the interpretation of dreams. Auden's view - conditioned by his reading of psycho-analysis - was that unconscious and conscious narratives carry versions of meaning and that there is a dependable, structured importance to be extracted from both.

The centrality of Freudian ideas to Auden's early poetry cannot be overestimated, and his own essays and reviews collected and edited by Edward Mendelson in *The English Auden* contain all the clues needed by a critic to assemble a summary of his approaches to art and poetry in the university years. Naturally, this makes it seem as if one needs to decode Auden's work, and there is much of his poetry which depends on the reader's biographical and psycho-analytical knowledge, but as with so much literature of this kind, there is no necessity for 'total knowledge' of a poetic text.

Auden's attitudes, inner conflicts, and rebellion were described by Isherwood in his autobiographical book, *Lions and Shadows* (1938) in which Auden appears under the name of Hugh Wesson. His rebellion takes the form of a secret, childish one, asserting imagination above harsh reality. Isherwood's account of his own creation of the fantasy-world of Mortmere, written - with Edward Upward - is an expression of intellectual, whimsical dissent. It is a surreal world, anti-older generation and anti-establishment. Most important for Auden criticism, it typifies the schoolboy humour which tried to account for the constructions of the masculine in imperialist literature. The Auden generation were looking for a discourse which could mock and undermine without showing too transparently the writer's own deeper apprehensions about what Isherwood called 'The test' - that of being a man, going to war, building a home and so on. In *Lions and Shadows*, the plot of the Mortmere stories concerns 'the eternal conflict between the Rat's Hostel and the university system'. The Rat's Hostel being the home of the hated male characters in the narrative.

Auden, under the shadow of Eliot, could dip into such reserves of surreal revolt and transmute them into the expressive images of the early lyrics, or into the crazy love poems spoken by the dislocated voices of the inhabitants of the 'city' which is Auden's word for human community.

Berlin, Teaching and War

Auden was in Berlin from October 1928 to July 1929. Why did he choose this destination? His friend Isherwood puts it bluntly: to Auden, Berlin meant boys. The Kosy Korner Café, where English writers and aesthetes could socialise with working class German youths was a 'cultural' attraction. In this period, Berlin was the centre of bohemian decadence, but also as an adventurous, avant-garde place, almost a visionary centre from which to view a liberated lifestyle and a potentially more open-minded future, with, moreover, greater artistic freedom.

There was the Hirschfeld Museum and Institute of Sexology. There was the magnetically alluring cabaret where the conferencier was poet, comedian and political satirist in one. Popular art-forms rubbed shoulders with poetry and high art. There had been an attempted revolution there in the decade previous to Auden's arrival, and it was the city of Brecht. It was where the underworld of *The Threepenny Opera* existed alongside the pavement intellectuals' fraternities where philosophy was discussed over coffee and schnapps.

The urbane citizenship of the artistic community always attracted Auden. His interest in the psychology of Homer Lane and John Layard also meant that he could talk and write with equally challenging subversion to the expressions of the Europeans: the liberated, free-thinking groups who hated the bourgeois above all else, as the enemy of progress, freedom and creativity. D. H. Lawrence's work and ideas also had an impact on him at this time. Auden read *Fantasia of the Unconscious* (1923). He used Freud's ideas on pleasure and pain to explain the otherwise inexplicable, whether in life or art. His friend John Layard tried to kill himself and failed, Auden being a witness to the bloody, tragedy-farce. Isherwood's ideas about 'The Test' and the power of suffering to renew and recreate the self are a factor in Auden's changing thought in his Berlin period. His later reading of Kierkegaard's treatise *Fear and Trembling* confirmed the value of human suffering as a point for seeing the human condition afresh, linking it to faith - but without puritanism.

11

He was publishing poetry that would quickly establish a high reputation. In *Poems* (1930) and in *The Orators* there is a similarity to Isherwood and Upward's 'The Enemy' who were - in fact - the establishment at Cambridge and everything they represented as seen through the eyes of the young. They were figures who appeared to have stopped thinking and to have blocked out true feeling from their lives. This, combined with his own uncertainties, led to prolonged enquiries into the nature of love in his poetry. Auden was interested in the reasons for the sense of despair, loss and futility around him: the failure to live - detectable in the spiritually-impoverished inhabitants of Eliot's *Waste Land*. He and his peers were trying to establish meaningful lives in the aftermath of the great carnage of 1914-18.

Auden returned to Britain in 1930. Teaching at the Larchfield Academy in Scotland, and the epiphany on the lawns of the Downs School in 1933 caused him to reclaim his Christian faith. The view that the joker in Auden, the whimsical farceur, was one expression of joy and celebration of the living of the present moment has some substance; it does at least explain his abiding interest in light verse. He revelled in action, in being busy and alive through responding and giving to others. He was active in many areas in the 'Thirties: both political and spiritual. To be a writer committed to political explorations was the order of the day, and this matched his growing ambitions as an artist.

He edited the anthology *The Poet's Tongue* with John Garrett; he was working with the GPO Film Unit in 1935-6, notably on the documentaries 'Coal face' and 'Night Mail'. He met Benjamin Britten, the composer, in this period as well.

Side by side with his celebration in life is the awful, negative experience in Iceland in 1936, when he saw a whale-slaughter on a massive scale. Several questions need to be asked about Auden at this time. For example, how did the experiences of man's inhumanity to man and to the creatures of God's universe in Iceland, Spain and Manchuria relate to his revision of belief at that time? What is the link between his poetic statements and his philosophic readings and speculations?

The use of heroic stereotypes in his works need some comment here. They are partly a conscious attempt to produce thought about being 'a man'- a preoccupation of many of the writers who 'missed out' on the chance to 'prove' their masculinity in the Great War - and also a contrast with the malaise of Auden's own peers and contemporaries - caused by the rise of Fascism.

Several people and places influenced him in a variety of ways in the 'Thirties. His work in the Spanish Civil War, under the auspices of the Spanish Medical Aid Committee, was short-lived but there he met people very different from himself, and saw the types of men who still needed 'The Test' Isherwood had written about. He also had new intellectual contacts such as Charles Williams, novelist and Christian theorist. He went to the Sino-Japanese war in Manchuria in 1938, with Isherwood, with whom, as a result, he wrote *Journey to a War*.

In January 1939, he arrived in the U. S. A. with Isherwood. Evelyn Waugh pilloried them as the characters Parsnip and Pimpernel in his novel *Put out more Flags* as 'rats leaving the sinking ship' and Auden was strongly criticised for his departure at that moment in European history. There are complex reasons for this desertion; perhaps he was running away from responsibility and from the Englishness in him. An inner hostility to his own homosexuality and the difficulties of expressing his sexuality in England, cannot be ruled out.

In the USA.

Auden met his lover, Chester Kallman, after a reading he had given with Isherwood in April 1939. He moved in the circle of political emigrés from Nazi Germany and did an increasing amount of literary journalism, lecturing and public readings.

He started taking the amphetamine Benzedrine at this time and did not come off the drug until the 1960s. But his general creative and scholarly habits were satellites around the planet of Kallman. Auden's love for him was a transcendent experience, as expressed in the poem, 'Law, like Love' and writers have discussed at length what their relationship was in terms of the generated influences on Auden's poetry:

'Although I can at least confine
Your vanity and mine
To stating timidly
A timid similarity,
We shall boast anyway:
Like love I say.'

This recurrent insistence on experience being only 'like' love is a discordant note, hinting at an uncertainty behind the apparent confidence of the language.

What strikes the reader about Auden in the 'fifties is how much he took on a dazzling range of forms, all with intellectual enquiry as their purpose, whether satire or love lyrics, essays or musical libretti. Underlying all this, however, was a set of dialogues concerning the private and the public sense of self. How often in Auden's poetry do we find a need to break conventional form? This is because he needed to innovate, to challenge and to maintain his status. Often he mixes contrasting discourses also, and making prose poetic *and* poetry prosaic. The poem, 'Memorial for the City' epitomises this characteristic. It has the diverse rhetoric of Eliot and the symbolic power of much of the best American lyricism of Robert Lowell, but its intellectual toughness overcomes the showy display of learning. The discipline of the poem's form helps to keep the thought coherent, reflecting pre-composition planning and speculation.

There is always a sense of history in Auden - often in the sense that Thomas Hardy perceived it - as a constantly present layering of human experience: bedrocks of feeling and passion, anger and discontent beneath us, as in Hardy's sketch of a church with his poem, 'Her Dilemma' (1866) which shows skulls lying under human discourse. Auden's later poetry has this kind of awareness - quasi-mystical but strongly linked to human circumstances.

In the 'Fifties Auden became very much the 'sage' and the public man, lecturing at a series of colleges, and being made Professor of Poetry at Oxford. His inaugural lecture at Oxford was 'Making, Knowing and Judging' (included in his book, *The Dyer's Hand* in 1963). At Oxford he was clearly in his element: the tutorial and the common room fed his urbanity and combative wit, and his sheer love of talk. His circle of acquaintance widened.

He was also socialising - and drinking - at his home-base of Ischia where he had been settled with Kallman. But, after being awarded the Feltrinelli prize of 33,000 dollars, Auden moved to Austria, buying a farmhouse at Kirchstetten. In the last ten years of his life drugs, drink and tobacco were obviously having a deleterious effect on his general health, but although the critical reception of his poetry was mixed, he worked enthusiastically on a variety of projects, including the libretto (with Kallman) of Henze's *The Bassarids* in 1963, and a translation of Goethe's *Italian Journey*, along with the usual workload of editing and lecturing.

He was affected by the massive political events of the sixties. His poems reflect his interest in, and concern with, the exercise of power in both its subtlest and its most comprehensive manifestations. His sagacity and morality are still present, soaking the lyrics like water on a dishcloth, but his public life gave him fresh outlets for talking about morals and politics.

It was in the late 'Sixties that a wider recognition of Auden's influence and achievement really began. There was a BBC documentary on his work; he gave the T. S. Eliot Memorial lectures at Canterbury, went to the London Poetry International, and was generally appraised and acknowledged. Monroe Spears' collection of essays in 1964 for Prentice Hall marked a definite perception of his status as a poet and of his centrality in the line of important poets following Eliot.

The public persona was reinforced by his appearance; his deeply-lined face was, apparently, caused by a specific disease (Touraine-Solente-Gole Syndrome). A comparison of photographs taken in 1962 and 1972 reveals an astonishing change in his physical appearance, the illness displaying symptoms of accelerated ageing in that decade. Yet there was something of a rugged, embattled public persona based on his wizened appearance. He looked as if he had lived in the fullest sense, his face marked by striations just as in his beloved rocky landscapes, and he came to represent a voice and a stance about poetry, textualising its importance in a secular age, as if wisdom did, after all, come with hard experience.

In his last years a collection of prose was assembled, including *A Certain World*, a commonplace book. The habit of keeping quotations and notes of special interest to the writer goes back to the Elizabethan age, and it is perhaps a sign of a dilettante, but in Auden's case, the book is a collection of miniature essays interspersed with extracts from his reading.

Auden was active to the last, travelling and working in both Britain and the USA. He died after giving a lecture in Vienna, on the 28th September, 1973. He had helped to make poetry seem significant in an age when, increasingly, space needed to be made in cultural discourse for the fundamental human values he so powerfully celebrated. More important perhaps, he also refused to be anything other than honest in all his statements on the human condition, never leaving out the trivial, absurd aspects of life: many of his self-portraits are similar to the Theatre of the Absurd of Beckett and Pinter.

II THIRTIES THEMES

When one contemplates the 'Thirties, particularly with the aim of understanding the writing of that decade of wars, it is useful to bring to mind its persistent images. The 'Thirties inaugurated the documentary which is vital to understanding one of the cultural and artistic impulses of the period, and indeed 'facts' are what imbue our imaginations now, looking back. Popular media constructions of the 'Thirties are of the fact of a world war at the end of the decade. Other images such as poverty, political turmoil, debate about class, the decline of the British Empire all gather around popular media constructions as well.

Mention the 'Thirties in Britain and we have the Jarrow Crusade, young men going to Spain to fight for principles, Orwell going to Wigan Pier to investigate the hidden lives of the working class. It was the time of the Mass Observation movement, when England was documented to the last degree to find out what the nation was doing to produce and to relax. It was the decade in which the middle class youth first began to define, with any palpable meaning, their inherited guilt. The intellectuals of that time were mostly concerned with their position on that great, puzzling borderland between liberal England of cricket, country hikes and Church of England hymns on the one hand, and a sense of being part of an enigmatic modernity on the other - a young voice with new forms with which to express dissent. So many of Auden's imaginative motifs, through much of his poetic artifice, are about borderlands, both real and metaphorical.

If particular facts must be assembled for special significance, then it could be noted that in 1930 Auden published his first slim volume, called simply *Poems* and Ramsay MacDonald led the first Labour government. At the end, in 1939, Auden went to the war in Manchuria and nuclear fission was discovered. On September 3rd, Britain declared war on Germany. By way of cultural contrast, Housman's collected poems were still selling very well and T. S. Eliot had declined from the avant garde figure who wrote *The Waste Land* in the 'Twenties into an Anglican High Church, élitist and reactionary thinker.

A critic coming to the works of W. H. Auden needs to be reminded that the so-called representative writers of the decade are perhaps only so because we have revised our perceptions radically in the light of new theories. Nevertheless, to read Auden's poetry is to follow a perspicacious intelligence into areas of thought and feeling that clarify the perplexities of his generation.

Is it possible to find a typical 'Thirties poem? The age of the documentary and of class awareness puts before us a poetry that is direct and 'about something' rather than about poetry itself. Stephen Spender's poem, *Pylons* is often quoted in this context as the opposite of anything romantic or too removed from everyday life. But this is a simplification. Auden's early poetry makes it clear that poets in this period had to address some 'issues' which would not go away. Principally, these were about rethinking English identity and culture , and the social relationships springing from these, in an age following the Great War and in anticipation of our running away from another war with Germany. Questions about masculinity, about living honestly and free-thinking were prevalent amongst the culturally aware.

It was also a decade in which the literature of escape was ubiquitous. Travel writing became not only popular but almost obligatory for any established writer to attempt. But escape from the stultifying Englishness Auden's contemporaries reviled so much could also be achieved in the imagination. Literature about ways of escape from narrowness, insularity and acceptance of the average was immensely popular. It was an age of parables about escape into more authentic, fulfilled lives; of noble causes and revisions of heroic ideas. On the stage, in fiction, in art and poetry - escape from the authority of the last generation's folly - was mandatory for the young writer.

The poetry which Auden helped to establish was consequently confronting issues that seemed to really matter. What Arnold Kettle called 'impure' poetry became acceptable. In other words, poetry that, in Hugh MacDiarmid's words 'Cuts the cackle' and makes important perceptions and observations became popular. This is not to say that Auden's poetry is never 'difficult'. In fact, the middle class, Oxbridge poets were also writing in the milieu of modernist experimentation and so there are still some challenging stylistic devices to unravel. Yet, Eliot's *Waste Land* had shown Auden and others that one's private, inner landscapes of feeling were just as legitimate artistically as a social commentary on the ills of the nation. There was still very much a 'two Englands' issue at the time - one of the rich and one of the poor - but also 'two identities' jostling for supremacy in the spirit of the middle class poet.

With these references in mind, perhaps there is a 'typical' Auden 'Thirties poem which can be used as a touchstone when reading others in his body of work. This is *The Bonfires* (1931) which has the essential Auden ingredients of a nameless, unnerving landscape which may be in the subconscious or may be rural England under threat from some unnamed menace. The first stanza is rural imagery immediately undermined by a paradox: 'the fortified farm' in a 'strange valley'. The stanzas build on this, with references to a 'dark squadron' and:

'The sound behind our back
of glaciers calving'

which is an early example of his ability to alarm and create unease in the reader by imposing anarchy upon order neatly and deftly in a short, concise lyric. The last stanza refers to a 'double traitor' and ends on a resonant ambiguity:

'To time the double beat
at last together.'

'At last' being either after a period or finally, with an apocalyptic nudge towards a terrible finality.

It is a simple poem on the surface, carrying no weight of abstract diction or philosophic questionings. We need no reference book to decipher anything. Instead, it forces us to enquire into the potential meanings of words we have spoken and read thousands of times before in a way that manufactures an elusive and indefinable threat to a comfortable cultural imagery.

The Orators

If a critic needed to focus on a text that exemplified the 'Thirties interest in the ideas of Freud and the unconscious, *The Orators* would be that work. It has the qualities of a dream sequence mixed with adolescent humour and strengthened by the addition of a broad attack on the establishment and on authority figures. It is formless, multi-generic and shows evidence of the writer's infatuation with the modernist eclectic approach of composition.

Yet beneath the surface jokes and childish whimsicalities there is a real sense of the 'Thirties *Angst*: the feeling of waste and futility which pervades much of the literature of the time. It is self-indulgent excess united to an attempt to make private humour part of the fabric of satire - seemingly expected of a bright young intellectual, and to that extent 'conventional'.

Its dream-like qualities are the most frustrating aspects of the work, but one idea does not integrate the flow of speculation and images - the 'condition of England' material - which interested so many thirties writers. Isherwood and Upward invented their imaginary Mortmere for instance, discussed earlier, and they referred to authority figures and college 'hearties' at Oxbridge as 'The Enemy'; Auden brings this into the image of a mentally constructed England that he attacks:

> 'Of the enemy as philosopher. Talking of intellect-will-sensation as real and
> separate entities. The Oxford don: "I don't feel quite happy about pleasure"'

There are several descriptions of the 'Enemy' in the work, all with the usual in-jokes about academic interests and often referring to the generation gap. The jokes even go so far as to mention, 'A beauty, a bone setter, a curate from Kew'. The bone-setter was a standard joke in Evelyn Waugh's fiction too. It would all be an in-joke.

The overall impression of *The Orators* is that of fragmented chaos. But the poetic elements redeem it. The odes in Book III attempt to crystallise much of this thinking. A section of Ode IV puts one central theme explicitly, after asking questions about 'our proletariat' and telling us that the upper class 'won't pass', we have:

> 'Who will save?
> Who will teach us how to behave?
> . . . . We're getting a little tired of boys,
> Of the ninny, the mawmet and the false alarm'

(mawmet = an idol or a puppet)

In Ode V to his pupils there are some inspired clarifications of some of the confusion of the prose section of the work:

'Boy, the quarrel was before your time, the aggressor
   No-one you knew.'

but there is still Auden's version of deserted land, a terrain of futility and negation, as if awaiting the redemption of the new leader or a moral enlightenment:

'Work has been stopped on the powerhouse; the wind whistles under
The half-built culverts.'

What we have then - in this early work- mixing monologues, lyrics, lists, diagrams and parodies- is almost a pastiche of *The Waste Land*. In a sense, it is that poem without the gravity and the ambition, made into a tour de force of juvenile exuberance. Only occasional gems appear in the mountain of verbiage. Yet in the spirit of the attack and in the verbal dynamics, the roots of Auden's most successful 'Thirties poems are visible. The problem for the critic is put well by Frank Kermode and John Hollander. When they included *The Wound* from *The Orators* in their anthology of modern British writing, they hinted that it could refer to a 'condition of sinfulness that a Christian would equate with his very humanity' but added that 'Auden did not give his own text' that meaning. In other words, like all inchoate works of a singular complexity, *Orators* has several levels of interpretation, and the fact that Auden can include an airman figure (clearly symbolic of a certain element of freedom) only invites these multiple readings.

Iceland and Lord Byron

In a review of Laurence Housman's book about his brother, the poet, *A. E. Housman: A Memoir,* Auden discussed the two identities inside the poet. He asks, 'Can man only think when he is frustrated from acting and feeling?' The review is deeply concerned with issues about the poetic temperament at a time when the place and function of the poet in society was undergoing fundamental revision. Auden develops his question into this dichotomy:

21

'Does life only offer two alternatives: you shall be happy, healthy, attractive, a good mixer, a good lover and parent, but on condition that you are not overcurious about life. . . .'

This is enlightening with regard to a turning-point in Auden's life, discussed in depth by Richard Davenport -Hines' excellent biography, and the focus here is on Auden's Iceland experience. Auden and MacNeice went to Iceland in 1936 and the resulting travel book, *Letters from Iceland,* contains Auden's long meditative poem of personal and social commentary, *Letter to Lord Byron.* There is a great deal of interest here to the critic approaching Auden's work. Tom Paulin, in an essay which examines some of the moral dimensions of Auden's writing and thinking at this time, suggests that the poem explores the frontier between the 'civic poet' in Auden and the poet who contemplated Lord Byron and all he stood for with awe and a certain respectful fear tinged with suspicion:

'Auden values the civil space highly and therefore he has no wish to be overwhelmed by the sterile mysticism of a giant mountain. . . . . and conformity and stability involve a loss.'

Paulin also stresses that 'the social responsibility of the artist is a virtually obsessive theme in Auden's criticism'. Much of this is related to guilt and a sense of inadequacy. The poem playfully juggles with these contrasting roles:

'His sense of other people's very hazy,
His moral judgements are too often crazy,
A slick and easy generalisation
Appeals too well to his imagination.'

So placing the poet in a lower order of artist than the novelist who attempts a more comprehensive scrutiny of humanity. But Paulin goes further, and links the choice of Lord Byron as the recipient of the letter to the cult of the aristocratic hero - which may be seen as much in Yeats as in the Nazi ideology - to Romanticism. The connection between the two may seem bizarre, but certainly there is a defence of English reticence, small-sized acceptance of art and Augustan harmony in Auden's dialogue with Byron:

'Parnassus after all is not a mountain
Reserved for A1 climbers such as you;
It's got a park, it's got a public fountain.'

This suggests that Auden wants to write for everyone, openly against any in-crowd or élite in art.

Letters from Iceland contains several layers of self-revelation. It is very much a commonplace book for Auden. He relates the experience repeatedly to a European centre of sensibility and artistic expression. 'Alone in Iceland you are alone indeed and the homeless, undisturbed wilderness gives something of its awful calm to the spirit.' Auden seems to relish an encounter with a culture close to ideas of the physical or even brutal element in life:

> 'All Cézanne's apples I would give away
> For one small Goya or a Daumier.'

He refers here to Goya depicting the horrors of war in the Spain of the Napoleonic War, and also, especially interesting in the context of the urbane Auden, to Daumier's cartoons and caricatures of de-humanised city dwellers in Second Empire France.

Auden's reaction to Iceland and his musings on the art of poetry to Byron provide a manifesto about the kind of poetry that is needed in order to have a social impact. Paulin says that Auden is discovering the dangers inside what we conventionally think of as 'civilisation' and indeed that questioning is there from the first lyric in Auden's *Collected Poems.*

Love and Belonging

Anyone reading Auden's poetry in the 'Thirties and 'Forties would be sure to notice the frequency of the word 'love' in the lyrics, repeatedly and with varying shades of meaning and inference, love becomes the central determining agent of his active sensibility. Richard Hoggart noted that this was a voyage of discovery, in which Auden is thinking through exactly what love means to him, in its broadest sense. The concept seems to be used in a personal way, and definitely not in the sense of romantic love. In his commonplace book, published as *A Certain World,* we have this startling statement:

> 'No notion of our western culture has been responsible for more human misery
> and more bad poetry than the supposition initiated by the Provençal poets. . . . that

a certain mystical experience called falling or being in love is one which every normal man and woman can expect to have.'

Various perspectives on exactly what version of love is meant in the poems could be provided, including Christian lines of thought and philosophic ones too, but essentially it describes a redemptive power within humanity: an integral part of a moral instinct. One of the most arresting examples of his explorations of the concept is in a poem at the close of the Iceland book, *Letter to William Coldstream Esq.*

'O stretch your hands across the sea'
The impassioned lover cries,
'Stretch them towards your harm and me
. . . . . The greater the love, the more false to its object
Not to be born is the best for man. . .'

and this should be placed beside these lines in the closing section of *Letter to Lord Byron:*

'My home then was professional and 'high'.
No gentler father ever lived. I'll lay
All Lombard Street against a shepherd's pie
We imitate our loves:'

The first hints at the extremes: the love of the metaphysical poetry that made him shudder. It is the love at the centre of an imbalance an escape from the mundane, faithful love expressed through service - as in his own middle class home. The first is destructive, leading to the Romantic sublime of being defined by capacity for emotional life. The second is as described in Gray's *Elegy* with its domestic, small-scale focus: 'They kept the noiseless tenor of their way'. In other words, it is private, internal, reserved.

Running through dozens of poems in this period, we have the concept of love as the classical *agape* : charitable love for mankind, not eros - the erotic imperative. *Agape* is a force for internal order, when properly understood. In the landscapes of his England, lovers and the abstract love are there as a fixed element in the course of human experience:

In the *Twelve Song*s written in 1936-38, we have a series of statements and questions, all testing out some approaches to the understanding of what we mean by the word. The most anthologised are the lyrics numbered XII and IX . Number XII could be a 'Sixties performance poem, toying with everyday ideas and observations, witty and vibrant, building up a series of questions to:

'Will it come like a change in the weather?
Will its greeting be courteous or rough?
Will it alter my life altogether?
O tell me the truth about love.'

The whole sequence deals with sublunary love: the love observed within the family, framed in constructs about duty, necessity and the romantic code of politeness, courtship and ritual. It is, above all - socialised love - made definable by action. In XI a Roman soldier meditates on Hadrian's Wall and thinks of home:

'The mist creeps over the hard grey stone,
My girl's in Tungria, I sleep alone.'

and what happens repeatedly is that Auden purposely uses the inflated language of the heterosexual, male-centred discourse of love in the English lyric. He uses it to undermine and to respect at the same time, often to point out its limitations as a view of what love is. This is because, partly, he wished to defend a higher homo-erotic love as instanced in the work of Plato. So we take the familiar discourse of affection and expressed passion as a culture-sanctioned ritual, only to think again about the emptiness inside the voice who speaks to us. This is seen clearly in poem IV, a poem of rejection following contentment, where the unloved of Auden's mental terrain of despair remain, waiting some kind of test that time will bring: the lovers around the pair in question are 'with hostile eyes',

'In pairs on every bed,
Arms round each other's necks,
Inert and vaguely sad.'

These notions relate in many ways to Kierkegaard's - one of Auden's favourite writers. In Kierkegaard's philosophic essay *Fear and Trembling* the writer says some interesting things about love and heroism that are relevant to Auden's conceptions at this time. First, he insists that there must be an eternal consciousness in man - that we must give a purpose and meaning to experience. The poet has a special role in this:

> '(God). . . . shaped the hero and the poet or speech-maker. The latter has none of the skills of the former, he can only admire, love, take pleasure in the hero. Yet he too, no less than the hero, is happy.'

and (of the poet):

> 'If he remains thus true to his love. . . . he is united with his hero. . . who in turn has loved him just as faithfully, for the poet is, so to speak, the hero's better nature.'

If we read Auden's poetry of love as a series of descriptions of this expression of a striving to find a love that is as fulfilling as the airman's life in *The Orators* then we have some idea of the magnitude of Auden's ambitions for his moral ideas.

There is no clearer example of all this thought than 'As I walked out one Evening' in which a detached voice from an urban setting is given the Metaphysical expression of the overstated credo of erotic love in lines such as

> 'I'll love you till the ocean
> Is folded and hung up to dry
> And the seven stars go squawking
> Like geese about the sky.'

The first five stanzas compare in this to Marvell's great poem 'To his Coy Mistress' but then the next five stanzas accelerate into the terrifying image of 'Stare, stare in the basin/ and wonder what you've missed' with its stark contrast of the lover and the unloved, each facing an absurd universe devoid of human meanings. This is partly because Auden did not completely rise to the concept of mature, responsible love. The dissonance here is very important in any reading of Auden, stressing his need to mix love and fear as concurrent emotions. This apparently perverse tendency in his work suggests his frequent failure to make anything successfully poetic out of an inner struggle. Finding Freudian explanations for such conflicts is, partly, an admission of his limitations as a poet. The last stanzas then elaborate on this bleak vision, ending with

> 'The lovers they were gone;
> The clocks had ceased their chiming,
> And the deep river ran on.'

In the end, then, what sort of belonging is reflected in the poems of this period? It is easy to see both extremes of a professed ardent affection of the lonely lovers caught up in horrendous, cataclysmic times, and the isolated, lonely individuals of the modern soulless city who somehow still see love as a redemptive force. It is as if Auden wants us to respond by questioning the constructs of 'love' as it has been conventionally defined and placed in a dominant ideology. His gay perspective, as with say, Forster or Isherwood, adds a further dimension to this view on life around him. This is not only one of detachment, but also a refusal to accept any of the platitudes that have formed a crust around the free flow of emotion which should be inherent in the expression of love. Gay perspectives on this dominant line of wit, conscious 'showing off' in the textually privileged male lover, can highlight its banalities. Auden rejoices in such intertextuality. It is interesting to note that his friend, Isherwood, does not approach this topic with such equivocation.

What Auden insists on placing before us - as readers aware of the lyric tradition of the male lover addressing the female beloved - is the marginality of his own 'love'. Time and again the poems which discuss love deflect the central emotion and search for metaphorical parallels, for what T.S. Eliot called the ". . . objective correlative . . ." described also by Martin Seymour-Smith as the ". . . objective equation for personal emotion. If the writer, in expressing an emotion about having killed his wife, composes a work about a toad eating dry, red eggs, then that situation is the objective correlative for his emotion at killing his wife."

In this way, Auden says that 'Law' is 'like love'. Love itself eludes a definitive statement. Clearly the point here is that there is unease, perhaps even a malaise, when he writes using the conventional literary constructions of loving and needing. The root of this unease is more than guilt, although this is part of it. More likely, his uneasiness is really about expressing 'the love that dares not tell its name' - which has no established discourse in literary English - within the canon of 'great texts' of heterosexual love. Our cultural processes marginalise homoerotic writing, despite our reverance for Shakespeare's Sonnets - in part homoerotic, as well as many other things.

An Intuitive Glance : the Ballads

Auden once referred to poetry as no more than an "intuitive glance". But he believed, with Jean-Paul Sartre, that the artist is also a citizen. If it is asserted that Auden was a satirist, then perhaps the most wise response is to admit to a need in him to reflect and comment, not necessarily to ridicule or abuse. The poetry that comes nearest to social commentary, hinting at the personality who was to become increasingly a version of the Augustan moralist, is most clearly seen in the ballads Auden wrote in 1937.

The poems concern three people: Miss Gee, James Honeyman and Victor. What they have in common is an oppositional detachment from the normal. Miss Gee is lonely but the scope of Auden's descriptions extends into much more than a story about isolation. The target is really puritanism of a particularly English kind:

'She bicycled to the evening service
With her clothes buttoned up to her neck'

and,

'She passed by the loving couples,
She turned her head away'

and Auden has fun with his Freudian interests again, noting the subliminal love for the vicar; a love that cannot be spoken, and the comment on her terminal cancer is put down to origins in lifestyles and temperaments - a subject which Auden rightly hints at being an expression of a superior, thoughtless imposition of some given 'explanation', incidentally relating to Homer Lane's ideas which influenced Auden and Isherwood, concerning sickness being spiritual and physical:

'Childless women get it.
And men when they retire;
it's as if there had to be some outlet
for their foiled creative fire.'

In the stories of James Honeyman and Victor also, there is this insistence that repression leads to the antisocial, an antipathy to the

28

common pool of love, opened to all in a healthy society. Honeyman's desire for knowledge with power leads to the ruin of what he loves. Victor's childhood repression and suffering creates a murderer. From today's perspectives, this all seems too-familiar, but it is the ballad form that gives these poems their extraordinary power to stimulate and develop further thought.

A ballad is a narrative form which handles concepts, philosophy, political ideas and so on, but links them neatly to the human situation. It carries a long tradition of folk-genre narrative which can relate to fundamental myths. The ballad uses approachable, colloquial speech. Auden does something with the form that had been done by Brecht in his songs: give surreal juxtaposition of ordinary and bizarre, so that we have a 'sensational' storyline similar to popular criminal narratives and folksongs in the eighteenth and nineteenth centuries. But with Auden's poems, one line can lead to a germ from which a whole profitable line of social criticism could be developed:

'They were married early in August.
    She said, "Kiss me, you funny boy";
Victor took her in his arms and said:
    "O my Helen of Troy. "'

which really invites a response which has to consider the nature of the lovers' imagination. The duality of our imaginative faculty as both creator and destroyer has to be resolved in terms of the poem, as he satirises their love.

But Auden's commentaries are very ambitious. Dozens of poems ranging from satire to ironic comment gather around his impulse to find an angle from which to represent his England as an example of the idea of community under threat from the new, exemplified as the city. He sees the city - the organic functioning of urban life - with its alienated individuals, as what interests him. A poem that extends this idea of the individual suffering ,unnoticed, like Gee and Victor, is *Musée des Beaux Art* which uses a favourite device of a panoramic landscape which diverts humanity. Just as the city makes anonymity and loneliness within crowds, so individual suffering is simply marginalised by events. The poem uses Breughel's painting showing Icarus plunging into the sea after the waxen wings that were to give him the power of flight have melted in the sun. A ship goes by, a farmer works on, regardless.

What is particularly interesting about this is the establishment of a tone and delivery which have become Auden's hallmark. Urbane, detached, a voice in the lyric first person which is so removed from the given situation that it is Augustan, eighteenth century, like Johnson or Pope:

'About suffering they were never wrong,
The old masters:. . . .

ending with a stanza bringing in the painting as if part of a conversation, when the narrative voice says,

'In Breughel's *Icarus* for instance: how everything turns away
Quite leisurely from the disaster. . . . . .'

What we have here is a poetry of dual identity. We sense the writer's presence as a contemporary in feeling, but the second voice gives a tone that distances us from the real in a way that invites all readers to be philosophers, to remain human but also observers of the human. Auden's intuitive glance is often far more a sustained stare.

In the 'Thirties, then, Auden was establishing a certain identity as a poet and writing a body of work that was soon seen as distinctive. In the Auden double number of the periodical *New Verse* there is a concept of style which is in need of the word Audenesque, and the issue was advertised with the pun Vin Audenaire. However one might try to describe what was unique in Auden, the end result is indisputable: a poetry which reflects a scrutiny of man somewhere between Hobbes' famous definition - 'The life of man is nasty, brutish and short' and Swift's comment on satire that he hated mankind but 'loved Tom, Dick or Harry'. Poetry for Auden had a duty to preserve and celebrate what is essentially human: whether of hope or despair. But *repeatedly* he undermines his art, putting it second to that of the novel. In his poem, *The Novelist* he says

'The rank of every poet is well known;
They can amaze us like a thunderstorm,
. . . . . . They can dash forward like hussars.'

30

Auden had done that by 1940. He had amazed, and forced his contemporaries to revise their views of poetry, following the Georgian anthologies in the 'Twenties and the post-Brooke poetry focusing on England and neo-Wordsworthian praise of nature. He reminded readers that, in Pope's words. 'The proper study of mankind is man.' The coming years, after the move to the USA, were to see repeated attempts by Auden to explain how new threats to the centrality of love were to be contained and understood.

III POETRY AND PHILOSOPHY
from *New Year Letter* to *The Sea and the Mirror*

After his move to America, Auden's poetry becomes more and more a form of experimental discourse attempting to reconcile a string of different impulses towards order and community. The poetry is either in strict metrical form or in open, wide-ranging thematic categories, but the common factor lies in adapting philosophical and Christian ideas to the realm of poetry - a socially aware, political poetry as well as spiritual and cathartic.

New Year Letter, written in 1940 and dedicated to his friend Elizabeth Mayer, is one of the most direct statements of this search for both a sense of community with love as an anonymous base. Auden's poetry is often an attempt to define and describe this place from which the individual lover constructs alternative realities. Love is placed as a construction of harmony in microcosm, even when the greater world disintegrates. The poem is written in the mood of a return to Christian belief, and it reflects his wide reading in literature and philosophy. He struggled to reconcile such things as the presence of evil in the world and the nature of the individual life and conscience. Questions of how we should live in a good community (and what this is, exactly) were also clearly beginning to be influenced by cultural perspectives much wider than his own symbolic and allegorical images of England, although, he still says:

'England to me is my own tongue,
And what I did when I was young.'

which suggests that there has been a rethink on the question of the formative influences on him as man and as artist. As Richard Davenport -Hines notes, the *Letter* was 'followed by eighty-one pages of prose notes and extracts. . .'. Auden was trying to bring together several strands of thought around these fundamental questions of being.

It could be argued that humanities study has always focused on the questions of how we are to understand ourselves as individuals and as citizens, and that most of the great thinkers on these topics have been polymaths - people of wide learning. Auden aspired to be a great thinker - combining aspects of literary knowledge with interests in other, broader areas of thought such as anthropology, sociology and science. The poem ranges from discussions of Rousseau and Marx to theological debate. The lines are also interwoven with words and phrases in Latin, French and German, with Greek terminology also interspersed. Yet amazingly, the poem stays readable, with most viewpoints being expressed neatly in the couplets.

The narrative is mostly in iambic tetrameter, though there are variations used. The effect is one of a poem firmly in the tradition of Augustan satire, after Dryden and Pope, but also of a narrative flexible enough to accommodate digressions, miniature studies, monologues and so on, all inter-relating the flow of ideas that Auden wishes to synthesise. At the centre of this is a reiteration of what Auden sees as a recipe for more than just survival: he asks when men will 'show common sense' and

'Establish a real neighbourhood
Where art and industry and *moeurs*
Are governed by an *ordre du coeurs?*'

This means surely that the *moeurs* - 'manners'/'morals' - should be interpreted as something more comprehensive and less inhibiting than the morality previously made communal in what Auden had attacked in his early poetry, and *ordre du coeur* in the last line implies a natural, inherent goodness.

Another strand in the poem is Auden's attack on mechanisation. What was (in *James Honeyman* for instance) a specific warning about the acquisition of knowledge, now becomes a repeated lamentation for the accelerated mode of life he sees around him.

'However we decide to act,
Decision must accept the fact
That the machine has now destroyed
The local customs we enjoyed'

and Auden widens the scope of his examinations into a humanistic elegy for the end of all the 'special tasks' begun by the Renaissance. As the poem unfolds a sense of how Auden wants to change focus regarding his perceptions of the individual's self-knowledge, comes out. The influence of Kierkegaard and that philosopher's insistence on the problem of relating the social admiration of the hero in a public sphere, with the key Biblical figure of Abraham, who is willing to sacrifice his son on God's orders, was relevant to Auden's thinking here. That is, Kierkegaard had used the story of Abraham to show the staggering potential of faith. The Danish philosopher's book, *Fear and Trembling* puts this in this way:

'The hero I can think myself into, but not Abraham; when I reach that height I fall down since what I am offered is a paradox . . . . Philosophy should not and cannot give us an account of faith. . .'

Auden tries to resolve these questions in *New Year Letter* by interweaving ideas from his various sources. For instance, he writes of Free Will in terms of an Existential line of thought:

'Hell is the being of the lie
That we become if we deny
The laws of consciousness and claim
Becoming and Being are the same.'

We are given free will, and it is possible that the most valid choices entail suffering rather than pleasure or gratification. Thus, Auden arrives at the position at which freedom taken to extremes invites destruction, misery and despair:

'Whichever way we turn, we see
Man captured by his liberty.'

In finding his way to the compromises at the end of the narrative, Auden has also reinforced the place of art and poetry in this fight for self-knowledge, when removed from the immediate scene of knowledge through suffering. Auden fills his lines with references to baroque music, art and culture. It is as if he is finding reassurance in the art of an age when the divorce between artistic humanism in theory and human misery in reality was easily perceived. That paradox was, of course, just as clearly observable at the time this poem was written - in the first year of the World War Two he had watched progress from afar in terms that invite metaphors such as:

'The situation of our time
Surrounds us like a baffling crime'

and,

'The bleeding tyrant dragged through all
The ashes of his capitol.'

So is there a statement in this long, ambitious succession of witty and incisive couplets that gives the reader some help in resolving anything in Auden's thought? Critics have thought the poem a mess and a failure, merely a confusing hash of half-digested theology and philosophy from a man who was more perplexed by the war, and what it signified, when removed from the immediate scene of conflict. But surely, there is something crucial about this metaphor which prefigures one of Auden's great achievements, In *Praise of Limestone*? In a section in the *Letter* which he centres on '. . . the human creature we / must nurse to sense and decency':

'Those limestone moors that stretch from BROUGH
To HEXHAM and the ROMAN WALL,
There is my symbol of us all'

and here, in this image, Auden finds an insight to unravel some complexities about self-knowledge and community: the valley has green and civil life near 'savage fells':

'From which original address
Man faulted into consciousness
Along the line of lapse the fire
Of life's impersonal desire.'

The implication is that we search for understanding of ourselves and of the human situation from a standpoint of inevitability, a process of formation like the geomorphology that creates the physical environment. The fault-lines direct and shape the individuals, but they are not what they seem to be- only a sense of an identity confined in a given element as we are shaped by society. Auden's conclusion of this poem is very much a synthesis of much of the thinking of the 'Thirties lyrics. His 'love' is now something with the moral dimension of our knowing ourselves through the rediscovery of that which was there before modernity shook the frame of beliefs that once held that Reason 'shaped our ends.' Joseph Conrad's image of life being fulfilling only if we 'in the destructive elements immersed' is relevant here. The final lines remind us that Auden had merely firmed up some thinking after this expedition into new territory:

'Our life and death are with our neighbour.
And love illuminates again
The city and the lion's den,
The world's great rage, the travel of young men.'

Uncivic Citizens

The question then arises: where does the work lead, after such soul-searchings and with the possibilities of new beginnings in a new world? One answer is that Auden looked closer at the relationship between the poet and his society and at the interlinking of the workable public life without compromise with one's inner, private life. Increasingly, Auden becomes interested in the nature of art and its part in transcendental experience- in contrast with the artist's poor, trapped earthly self, doing perfunctory duties- but also loving other humans.

Auden's interest in the private and public self can be partly explained by reference to the work ethic. In Dickens' novel, *Great Expectations*, the clerk Wemmick separates his home from the outer public world of employment and citizenship by having a drawbridge. His home is indeed his castle, and he lives there with his elderly relative. What more Audenesque image could there be than this? Wemmick is contributing to society; he represents a recognisable classification, but first in his life comes home and family. Dickens' theme of rising in the world through unearned income, contrasted with Joe Gargery's static self, remaining unchanged and directed by the necessity of honest toil, could be a symbol from Auden's metaphorical city. Dickens and Auden were both essentially poets of the new city: they recorded and inspected the nature of this self-made, new human being, brought about by the new capitalism.

Many of Auden's poems up to *The Sea and the Mirror* (completed in 1944) deliberate on such subjects. Obviously, sociologists and historians had been aware of such concepts of alienation and *anomie* for some decades before these poems, but such ideas were only entering literature through modernist ideas, read and considered only by a minority, perhaps even an élite. Marx's idea of alienation is that man is separated from the process of making things for others. The capitalist mode of production confines the worker to one operation, depriving him or her of the satisfaction which was formerly available to a craftsperson in the so-called cottage industries. This idea broadened into several other applications and meanings, all related to the changes impressed on people by urbanisation and mechanisation. So the theory goes, if you accept it. Auden's writing does accept this, and it is difficult to disagree. *Anomie* was coined by the sociologist Emile Durkheim, and refers to a condition of despair and lack of an identity-sense which results from a negation of social cohesion and purpose. In other words, it is a kind of inner anarchy (literally meaning lawlessness). Auden's desire to see a cause for hope in the late 'Forties emerges from several feelings expressed from the late thirties through to *The Age of Anxiety* which are closer to the futility of anomie. For instance, in *The Unknown Citizen* he makes one of his clearest ironical statements about what the American sociologist David Riesman was to call 'The Lonely Crowd' (1950). The poem is a satirical obituary to anonymity, once again insisting through the ironies that the private, inner life has to regain a personal authenticity, a belief in being. The last two lines reinforce the power of Auden's use of pronouns to represent the edifice of the inhuman state:

'Was he free? Was he happy? The question is absurd.

Had anything been wrong, we should certainly have heard.'

and the poem's effects are punched home through a forceful sarcasm constructed around the terrors of euphemism:

'Both Producers Research and High-Grade Living declare

He was fully sensible to the advantages of the Instalment Plan. . .'

The poem is a typical instance of Auden dazzling to understate, using an impersonal, detached voice. But in the 'Forties he was becoming increasingly at home with the laments for the waste of life by the crass, the materialistic and the narrow-minded. The 'Little Man' still has virtues that live on beyond the chaos of world war and internal disintegration through the loss of all certainties.

In dozens of the shorter poems written in the 'Forties, Auden returns to these notions of how we are to authenticate our lives- give them sense and meaning. One answer is still the Christian one - to relate love to suffering in an imperfect world. In one of the most successful of these, *Canzone*, Auden seems attracted to the style of the Metaphysical Poets. In the manner of John Donne or Marvell, he opens with a rhetorical question which seems to come from the process of thought 'overheard' by the reader:

'When shall we learn, what should be clear as day,
We cannot choose what we are free to love?

and he goes on to examine the nature of the desiring ego - our little self which has to see creation as if it is more important than the magnitude of the world and nature. 'The fluent satisfaction of our will' we see as the physical world.

In the third stanza we have the opposite: an account of the negation of certainty- a version of our will that is self-undermining. Auden uses the word melancholia as part of this - again very much associated with seventeenth century Metaphysical conventions. This other self, expressed as an anti-will, he links with a withdrawal of a vital force.

'To ruin and remember that we know
What ruins and hyenas cannot know'

This last image is of a type that can either enlighten or infuriate. Auden tends to use a type of imagery that is very similar to the 'conceit' in seventeenth-century Metaphysical verse: that is, a form of wit which uses a far-fetched metaphor to join apparently unrelated items together. With Auden, it is more a case of a suggestive image linked with another. Ruins and hyenas have certain qualities in common *only when* part of the stylistic fabric and syntax of a sustained passage packed with related ideas. In this way, the 'violent dogs' referred to earlier in the stanza relate to the hyenas. It takes intense concentration to follow Auden's thinking through his poetic structures.

Also in several poems of this period, Auden explores the metaphor of darkness and night with its biblical meaning of both sin and the soul's peace when a new kind of understanding is open. (The story of Nicodemus in the Bible). But in the concluding stanza of *Canzone* he adds the variation of a 'God of Love' to his already well-established references to love within the individual:

> 'Dear fellow creature, praise our God of Love
> That we are so admonished, that no day
> Of conscious trial be a wasted day.'

So here we have Auden revamping previous thought in a Christian form: a renewal of his now familiar questioning, but with a resolution similar to Metaphysical lyrics. This proper expression of love for others must join with will to overcome melancholy - keep the hyenas at bay. If we accept the idea of free will, then all versions of suffering have a place in the scheme of things:

> 'There must be sorrow if there can be love.'

In the poem's development we have followed a kind of disputation: a process of wild logic that is an exercise in self-persuasion. But the success of the poem is in its handling thought and feeling as they emerge. The reader shares the effort to think - and either accepts - or disputes the conclusion. Free will, in the first line is 'clear as day' but we want this proved to us in some way, particularly if we have no Christian belief. Auden's poem does no more than accumulate the reasons for doubt, and although it is legitimate for a poet to insist that he does not provide answers, Auden's work does obfuscate, sometimes with a delight in obscurity.

Ultimately, poetry can only describe, perhaps, and Auden's aim is to describe a new set of symptoms, but the illness is always the same: whether a sickness of the soul, rejection, isolation, or absolute despair.

The Sea and the Mirror

The Sea and the Mirror is a mixture of poetry, prose and song which develops monologues from the characters of Shakespeare's play, *The Tempest*. It is useful to give a few facts about this source first. *The Tempest* is classified as a 'late romance' (1610-11), one of a group of plays written near the end of Shakespeare's life when he wanted to express a view of man that could reconcile the conflicts of reason and emotion within him. In the play, there are extremes of human intellect, evil and bestiality, and we also have a view of love and marriage as a sacred union signifying the culmination of human happiness. One of Auden's most celebrated statements comes to mind here: 'We must love one another or die', which in this context surely means far more than a straight choice. The inference is that anything other than a commitment to another as a completion of yourself is a kind of death or emptiness.

Shakespeare is reflecting on the similarity of art to the meanings we impose on reality, whether these are religious, moral or political. That is, the natural desire to impose order and purpose on life is understandable, but life's fragility and indeterminate length may ruin such designs. Art can deal with this dilemma. In all his late romances amazing, irrational events convey a sense of wonder and awe. Man is depicted as a creature with infinite potential for happiness and love, but somehow is drawn fatally to despair, cruelty and destruction. The 'insubstantial pageant' of art Prospero refers to is his life, his reality.

Auden's development of some of these themes is in keeping with his earlier questions concerning our motivation towards negation and suffering. Shakespeare's is also a parable. Prospero, a former Duke of Milan whose place has been usurped by his brother Antonio, is now so learned after living in exile on his island, that he has mastered the magic arts. He has two servants, Ariel 'an airy spirit' and Caliban (cannibal?) a 'savage and deformed slave'. Prospero has tried to teach both, but with Caliban he has failed.

Prospero's daughter, Miranda, represents the sheer wonder that emanates from childlike innocence. The play concerns the shipwreck of Antonio and other 'men of sin' on Prospero's island, and Prospero's treatment of these is akin to a monitored experiment, arriving finally at a kind of redemption of all categories into some kind of humanity - except Caliban the beast-man- and this is obviously significant.

With this in mind, Auden's long prose monologue given to Caliban is clearly the crucial element in the work. The irony is that Prospero has taught Caliban to speak and Caliban, in *The Tempest* has said,

'You taught me language; and my profit on't

Is, I know how to curse. The red plague rid you

For learning me your language.'

Reading Auden's poem, the critic needs to keep in mind the context of the darkest years of the Second World War, and the perception of humanist thinkers that the dream of man's melioration - his gradual improvement - was destroyed. Victorian optimism that all would be well with a Christian creed and an Empire where right and goodness would be disseminated, was over-shadowed by the imperial slavery of countless millions of subject people from Russia to Africa: in a sense, Calibans. But also, Auden's perceptions about the loss of a true communal impetus in man and of a breakdown of inner selfhood raise questions about where art and poetry stand in all this. The poet Alan Bold once asked: 'After Hiroshima, you ask a poet to sing?' and there is something of this in Auden's stance.

But at a deeper level, the poem also allows Auden to include some personae - narrative voices - into the monologues which enable him to deliver provocative insights:

'I never suspected the way of truth

Was a way of silence where affectionate chat

Is but a robber's ambush. . . . .'

Prospero, in saying this, makes it clear that he too has much to learn, as he does in *The Tempest* through observing, overhearting and piecing together an artist's version of the humanity about him. In other words, Prospero - often seen as a persona for Shakespeare himself- or 'the artist' in general- is also in miniature the inner voice of the poet trying to understand the creator and his creatures: his own life and imagination.

Therefore, as Monroe Spears says, the poem investigates the mirror of art and the sea of life - reality. He also calls the poem a type of 'closet drama', but whatever the form, the sea metaphor does convey a shapeless, unknown mass: an infinite area of the unknown, from which

we deduce 'truths' simply from occasional, very small insights.
Each speaker expresses a view of life, from the drunkard's

> 'I was not looking for a cage
> In which to mope in my old age'

to Sebastian's:

> 'Right here is absolute and needs no crown,
> Ermine or trumpets, protocol or sword.'

Even Trinculo the jester (Latin: tricinium = dining room?) expresses his inner Angst: 'A terror shakes my tree / a flock of words fly out'. Auden reserves the clearest, most resonant image for Miranda untouched by life's complexities until she loves Ferdinand:

> 'So, to remember our changing garden, we
> Are linked as children in a circle dancing.'

Before Caliban addresses the audience in prose, we have been asked to understand the characters in the play as a series of individuals with a greater or lesser degree of an understanding of themselves- but they all attempt to express a reconciliation of life with death. In a sense, Caliban's ugliness and lack of true human form is nearer to death - a reminder of the Elizabethan notion of the cosmos in which creatures moving or dwelling in or near the earth itself are closer to the Devil's domain. Ariel flies in the highest element whilst Caliban drags his weight along the ground.

The object of Caliban's monologue is the division of art and life in a milieu in which 'culture' has defined the artist and limited the artistic vision to a particular pattern. Related to this is the artist's inner dichotomy -as Auden said of Housman - about the detachment of the poet from 'nature red in tooth and claw'. If the poet is a cultured, well-read, middle-class observer, keeping the Caliban in himself at bay, then what price the art and poetry? Caliban puts it like this:

> . . . and you have now all come together in the larger colder emptier room on this
> side of the mirror which does force your eyes to recognise and reckon with the
> two of us. . . .'

and he imagines the possibility of everything he represents being left alone to grow and change after nature's course to provide the poet with 'the good right subject'.

42

What Auden is dealing with, then, is the poet's quest to recreate 'life' and 'experience' through 'knowledge'. But that knowledge is limited and defined by a narrow conception of art: a cultural 'product' that excludes the unknown, the frightening, the base. When Auden insists on the vital creativity of suffering, he is hinting at the Caliban in us, just behind that 'mirror' of protection, which lies between us and a fuller knowledge of ourselves.

IV The Age of Anxiety

Poets, critics and theorists reflecting on poetry in the 'Thirties and 'Forties, became increasingly focused on that element in poetic discourse which uses myths, parables and allegories. For instance, in a popular Faber anthology, Michael Roberts says, 'Myths are more than fumbling attempts to explain historical and scientific facts; they control and organise feeling'. He argued that their function is 'symbolic as well as significant', and in that period, allegory had been widely used in prose and in drama. The novels of Rex Warner exploit this-as does the theatre of Rupert Medley- who was involved in the production of Auden and Isherwood's plays. It was an age that made great claims for the social use of poetry: Roberts adds, 'There is a relation between the personal and moral problem and the political and intellectual.'

Writers looked for new ways to relate these two aspects of socially committed poetry: the parable and the public-private parallel relationships. Auden unashamedly took up a didactic manner, and has sometimes been criticised for this ('the message is often mocked by the manner' says Stuart Hampshire). Auden insisted that 'The primary function of poetry. . . . is to make us aware of ourselves. . . . I do not know if such increased awareness makes us more moral or more efficient. I hope not.' This indicates how far we should take his didactic stance- not to any extreme but with an awareness of the uncertainty of the lyric 'I' in his poetry. In fact, is is possible to argue that Auden did not achieve this 'awareness' of himself or provide his contemporaries with such awareness, in his later writing. Only rarely does the clarity and acuteness achieved by the 'Thirties poetry gleam through.

Auden wrote *The Age of Anxiety* (1944-46) with some of these considerations in mind. But before an attempt is made to summarise and interpret this, the nature of allegory and didactic poetry needs to be explained. An allegory is a narrative with a secondary, implied meaning, like a biblical parable. The story of the prodigal son is 'about' something universal and deeply human, not simply confined to that specific relationship. An allegory will create such a framework, with a sub-text which the reader has to interpret, linking the 'surface' text to the sub-text. At its simplest level an allegory will point a moral. In the study of popular culture, for instance, it is clear that many television advertisements tell a story in order to sell a product through a sub-text. Analogously, an allegorical poem such as *The Age of Anxiety* can provoke thought and reflection.

Didacticism in art is a 'teach or preach' attitude expressed, in Auden's case in poetry (and prose). Criticisms of Auden are often based on the attitude that such poetry is out of place in an amoral age. Against this, the idea that poetry should convey one individual's response to social change always implies a moral stance. How far one can accept the moral element in Auden's philosophising is questionable. The existence of the moral stance is definite; where the problem lies is in how Auden's questions of the condition of being are relevant to his time. What is certain is that Auden created, with ingenuity and style, a range of personae - narrative and lyric 'speakers' which enable him to inhabit a character and an intellect in order to convey a response or suggest a trend.

In *The Age of Anxiety* he needed a form and he chose what he calls 'a baroque eclogue', and with the introduction of this type of terminology, we move on to another Auden: one we have seen fleetingly but who, by the late 'Forties, was increasingly emergent. Auden the Christian, fuses with Auden the self-doubting. The urge towards reassembling past certainties is at odds with the urgent need to interpret the modern urban condition of mankind. Giorgio Melchiori, in his study of 'mannerism in modern English literature', *The Tightrope Walkers*, says of Auden's middle period work:

> 'I think that Auden. . . . has actually detected the tendency in thought, feeling and style towards a stricter balance, a more symmetrical structure, and has tried to express it in the adjective baroque.'

This interest in classical form is a blanket to cover Auden's doubts about the truths of religion. His poems constantly provide eloquence about faith, but always to the point of loving the language and the learning more than any simplicity of faith or direct credo. For this reason, it now seems quite understandable that so many of his contemporaries took his words as somehow pronouncements.

In the visual and plastic arts, Baroque usually applies to forms which are exceptionally ornate and extravagantly done- it conveys also symmetry and balance in design but with minute elaboration - almost distracting detail. Auden's form and structure of this poem in a sense fulfils this definition, particularly in part one, and he also switches from dramatic effects to parody at times.

The other term, eclogue, stems originally from classical Greek literature and means pastoral. This means that the setting of poetry was conventionally rural, idyllic and often about love, the enjoyment of nature and a commentary on the simple fulfilment of such a lifestyle. There is a mythic, unreal quality about the genre, and in Virgil's poems, the *Eclogues*, perhaps the most famous set of poems with that name, the Latin used is far removed from everyday, functional Latin, as far as scholars may deduce. Eclogues and pastorals of various kinds have been used by English poets purposely to provide a satirical commentary on contemporary life, notably the corruption of court and public life. This spirit is in Shakespeare's *As You Like It*, for instance. But there is another function of an eclogue. The Dorset poet, William Barnes, for instance, used the form to stress the contrast between the local and the universal; it has been used to reaffirm the validity of localism and the way in which identity is related to a sense of place. Paradoxically, Auden's work has the added irony of being very much an urban text.

With all this background in mind, Auden's work is consciously ironical. The setting is in an American bar and the characters are run-down, despairing people at a moment of melancholy and dejection. They are described in this way:

> '. . . . . . Self-judged they sit,
> Sad haunters of Perhaps who after years
> To grasp and gaze in get no further than their first beholding. . . . . .'

Clearly, the 'Anxiety' of the title covers a wide range of potential application in the text. But Auden's essay on Kierkegaard sheds light on what he means: he lists things that 'If I take away from my sense of existence all that can become an object of my consciousness, what is left?' Only one thing is left, he says, 'A state of anxiety':

> 'For these states of anxiety or pride etc. . . . . are anxiety about existing, pride in existing, and I cannot stand outside them to observe them.'

And he goes on to express his ideas with regard to the Christian doctrine of the Fall, but there is a particularly interesting final part: 'Man fell through pride. . . . . to derive his existence from himself, and not through sensuality or any of the desires of his "nature".' Auden is clearly referring to the similarities between earlier, classic representations of the Fall from Eden and his contemporary intention: his interpretation of the modern urban world as a failure of humanity's construction. The backdrop for the allegory is one of a dystopia. In part three we have an imaginary vision of the future which is dream-like to the extent of being filled with the unnerving surreal landscape of another type of fall.

A summary of the sections of the work and their styles gives a useful overview of Auden's scheme:

Part One: In the bar A description of limbo, suspended life, waiting for being.

Style -   Alliterative pure stress verse, using kennings.

(A kenning is an early Germanic image which uses clusters of consonants and divides each line with a balanced syllabic harmony, as in Auden's:

> 'Flesh flusters that was so fluent till now,
> Stammers some nonsense, stops and sits down.')

Part Two: A summary of a variety of life-experience.

Style -   A three or four stress line. Still alliterative but dramatised, using prose links.
Auden 'orchestrates' the self-examinations.

Part Three: A journey into a wilderness and a vision of the future.

Style -   More dramatic, with a sense of the intimacy of monologue contrasted by a chorus.

This section also has a focus on a baroque garden, conveying the completion of their journey, but they are troubled and lost. They wake from a dream in the bar, then go to Rosetta's flat.

Part Four :	'The dirge' is a reflection on the need for a redemptive hero.
Style -	A lyric with Elizabethan conventions of elegy, with iambic stress.
Part Five:	The masque
	Rosetta and Emble embrace in the symbolic dance. All the cast give oracular commentary on the consequences of 'anxiety' as observed in a claustrophobic, sublunary world.
Style -	alliterative, four-stress line.
Epilogue:	The male characters return to their lives in the world of responsibility and normality. Each reflects on the impossibility of enlightenment. The atmosphere is Orwellian, a seedy '1984' milieu.
Style -	Prose links and a continuation of 2 or 3 stress lines.

An exhaustive study could be written, extrapolating the layers of stylistic devices in the work, but *The Age of Anxiety* is essentially a visionary allegory: a moral tale in dramatic form, in which we follow (from comedy to elegy) the modern consciousness from origins to present crisis.

In the first part, Auden makes Emble the notable philosopher, summing up then outsiders in a room:

'Estranged, aloof,
They brood over being till the bars close,
The malcontented. . . . .'

and he intersperses the dramatic present with the stereotype, mythic 'England of the mind' now in a receding past:

'I see in my mind a beseiged island
That island in arms where my home once was.
Round green gardens, down grooves between white
Hawthorn-hedges. . . . . .'

but America has provoked Auden to register a revised view of mankind's specialism in negation and destructiveness:

'The / bravura of revolvers in vogue now
And the cult of death are quite at home
Inside the city'

and the war across the ocean is reflected in a universal suffering: an inner voice of the spirit made real - reified - in the city:

'Lies and lethargies police the world
In its periods of peace. What pain taught
Is soon forgotten.'

This is one statement of the ideological centre of the piece; 'What pain taught' refers to the changeless, integral 'pain' of being alive - a spiritual weight, not a drive to external ruin and cruelty. Always in the setting, we have what many critics call the 'psychic or moral geography' Auden keeps inviting us to consider, thinking, as Auden said of the German poet, Rilke, 'Of the human in non-human terms'.

There are a few lines of thought which constantly recur in the major works such as *The Age of Anxiety* and one principal interest is the fact that our experience of ourselves is a mystery, but part of our search for meaning involves a recognition that part of our search relates to myth. This is often a version of archetypal experience. There are only occasionally glimpses of Auden's potential for conveying the depth of the interpretation of childhood and its privileged insights into beauty or meaning - as in Wordsworth. Auden is far more interested in a fresh perception of morality in a secular world. As Edwin Muir says in his autobiography:

'I fancy that even under dictatorships, where apprehension is a daily part of life, people have a spring of happiness, not from any privately nursed ideal, but simply from the society of friends, an inexhaustible, hidden source.'

A study of Auden's 'Forties poetry invites some answers to the question of the Freudian element in all this. If one discusses inner landscapes and moral structures in his narrative poetry, then it seems legitimate to ask just what is the psychological dimension. One reply is to refer to Auden's poem on the death of Freud (in September, 1939), *In Memory of Sigmund Freud*. Here, he makes large claims for Freud's achievement, having no doubts about the depth of modern society's search for a unity, a completeness of the self. Freud 'Went down among the lost people like Dante' and 'merely told/ the unhappy present to recite the past' but by the last five stanzas, Auden is talking about more than the exploration of the unconscious. He naturally relates our 'submerged' selves, in the familiar metaphor of 'the night' to a sense of deep loss. The final lines express it with the use of Greek deities:

'. . . . . . . Over his grove
the household of Impulse mourns one dearly loved:
Sad is Eros, builder of cities,
And weeping anarchic Aphrodite.'

Much of Auden's thinking about the nature of anxiety is here. In fact, Eros, God of physical love, the erotic impulse, creates in the 'made world' of our humanly constructed reality something notably different from any goddess of love in the abstract. This is a reckless, illicit, deceiving love, as it is selfish: against the rational order. Aphrodite was caught in a net with her lover, Ares, god of war, and exposed to ridicule. So there is a connection between destruction, lust, pleasure and gratification of the desires. Auden is suggesting that love creates and destroys, and is either communal or isolated. Of course, love has been the subject of political attempts at social control in twentieth century totalitarian states, and Auden seems to imply that the expression of romantic love is contrary to public harmony and identity. Indeed, there is some similarity here to Reich's notions of the results of the suppression of sexual desire, and in Auden's case, this reminds the reader yet again of Auden's study of Housman and the 'two poets' in him. This has been a convention of love poetry since Virgil:

'Pallas can keep her cities,
But let the woods beyond all else please you and me.'

(Eclogue II)

and John Donne expresses the idea succinctly:

'For love, all love of other sights controls
And makes one little room, an everywhere.'

Some of Auden's extensions of Freud's ideas, then, are linked to the destructive, self-seeking nature of love, paradoxically juxtaposed with the social impulse. The final section of *The Age of Anxiety* is dispersal, a fragmentation of community, and a return to the self from others, losing the fulfilment of the kind of love celebrated through his writing life.

Auden was searching for a way of defining the modern malaise. In several poems he gives us attempts at intellectualising his ideas of how we must *belong* in a different sense - adjusting our notion of what is human to comprehend what the twentieth century has done. The descent of man, imagined in dystopias such as Aldous Huxley's *Brave New World* and in George Orwell's *1984*, was open to interpretations ranging from the horrific to the pseudo-scientific. Auden looks plainly and honestly, with the perspective of a Christian who is never superficially moralistic. He is saved from preaching because poetry and art have a place in this new definition. Much of Auden's later poetry is an expression of this need to find a new configuration.

His poem *In Praise of Limestone* is one of his most widely assessed statements in this context. In varying ways, the poem describes the need to be divorced from any expression of our difference, our separateness from the constant process of change, of creative mutability to be seen in geomorphology. The opening lines ask us to accept this:

'If it form the one landscape that we, the inconstant ones,
Are consistently homesick for, this is chiefly
Because it dissolves in water.'

Again, Auden develops an evocative account of the underground, inner organic life of this scenery, only to contrast it with 'The light less public and the meaning of life/ Something more than a mad camp.' What develops is a transcendental vision, interpreting our freedom as an acknowledgement that we must understand the sub-human, that solitude which says to us,

'There is no love,
There are only the various envies, all of them sad.'

Auden once more lamenting the absence of true giving and *caritas*, or *agape* in humanity: the ability to love without selfishness and possession. Hundreds of talented artists and writers have been interested in articulating such thinking, but Auden's extraordinary vision of our being in a state of joy without envy or desire is one of the most powerful:

'. . . . . . . but when I try to imagine a faultless love
Or the life to come, what I hear is the murmur
Of underground streams, what I see is a limestone landscape.'

Which is in firm contradistinction to the Wordsworthian vision of nature which introduces divine instruction - a precept for happiness from a perceived grandeur - reflecting what is inside us. Auden is more concerned with a potential change in humanity, a fundamental reformation of how we live together and how we understand ourselves.

The baroque is one piece in this assortment of forms and discourses that recurs in the 'Forties poetry, as if Auden is using classical literature to evoke a view of nature to enlighten his own contemporaries' uncertainties as to their place in the nuclear universe. In other words, if they were to live under the shadow of the end, of the descent of man into self-destruction, what reminders of harmony and order were there to be accessed in the world of Virgil and Horace, of Greek pastoral and of pagan animism? The sequence of poems, *Bucolics* imagines some accounts of our loss to be described.

In *Winds* the line that could be a sub-text for the sequence is given: 'I am loved, therefore I am'. It is a metaphor for poetic inspiration, but Auden expands this into an affirmation of his belief that art and love share a particular urge to relate and belong. Every 'verbal rite' should be 'fittingly done' even when in dejection. The poem is a prayer to the human base - the substance which makes each an individual. Auden as a maker, a creator, is part of a process of constant recreation of meanings. 'A few dear names' are the significant human creations.

The sequence is a useful location from which to begin a study of a notable feature of Auden's later poetry: his interest in place and space - both personal and geographical. Several contrasting strands come together here, but there are three productive approaches to this: the convention of landscape and literature in English, the poetry of place and identity and finally, Auden's theme of *homo ludens* - man at play.

Conventions of landscape and literature

In Auden's poem *In Transit* he says:

'Somewhere are places where we have really been, dear spaces

Of our deeds and faces, scenes we remember
As unchanging because there we changed. . . . . .'

As Edmund Wilson noted, in America, Auden was dealing with 'the
discomforts and disquiets, crimes and myths' of the whole modern
world, and so we should expect a different viewpoint on the idea of
landscape as it is positioned in the English poetic traditions. *Bucolics*
does emphatically offer this. Each poem is a meditation on the human
geography we make and also the element which is forced on us by
necessity. Auden adds several ingredients which give the sequence a
mixture of humour, playful speculation and wisdom.

First, however, how has the poetry of landscape been established in
the English literary tradition? In the eighteenth century, the Augustans
were concerned with the way a natural panorama is transformed by
human interference. The view was that man should create an artificial
landscape that would reflect notions of social hierarchy and power -
e.g. Alexander Pope, but a later example of this is in Jane Austen's
Mansfield Park where the estate of Sotherton is 'improved' by being
landscaped. Wealth and status insist on nature being improved upon.

The changes of attitude in the Romantic movement brought about
significant developments in how people were to live within nature. In
the poetry of John Clare, for instance, the issue of depopulation from
the countryside through enclosure forces him to depict human misery
at the loss of what is dear about a special place, as he voices the
laments of dispossession for those workers who had no ability to
express such things.

Auden moves at a tangent from this, and uses ideas about our living
space which are more concerned with flippant and whimsical
comments such as,

'The trees encountered on a country stroll
Reveal a lot about a country' soul'

and insists that hills and heaths are for Romantics whereas
lakeside life is more civilised. In other words, Auden is purposely
writing pastiche here. Virtually all the solemn and serious themes to do
with the grandeur of nature are undermined. Even Arthurian legend is
subject to his reduction:

> 'The little lady of the glacier lake has fallen
> In love with the rare bather whom she drowns'

Auden's treatment of the idea of how a sense of place relates to self-identity is more interesting and more complex. He stands outside, detached from the traditions outlined above, giving a voice of jocular ordinariness, an antidote to the Wordsworthian transports at the sight of a particular place. An important insight into his approach to this is in *Plains*:

> 'Which goes to show I've reason to be frightened
> Not of plains, of course, but of me.'

and in a semi-comic manner, the whole sequence has hinted at the functions of self and place: 'If I were a plainsman I should hate us all'. The pronoun 'us' in this line is significant. It suddenly puts the whimsical description in a context of meaning; our environment does have a profound influence on us, and we must still put the idea of togetherness first. 'Us all' not 'them all' or 'the others' in hills or on shores.

The poetry of this period in Auden's life has been negatively judged as not being indicative of an integrated, coherent interpretation of life, with no steady thematic focus. This is short-sighted, since the theme of place and identity constantly recurs, and it is 'the city' that is in focus. A more important and accurate criticism would be that intellectualism is always integral to the poetic construction. *Memorial for the City* (1949) is very ambitious and it illustrates Auden's demands on the reader. The reader needs reference texts and is asked to inter-relate a string of historical allusions. Auden tries to maintain coherence by asking us to imagine our condition as in part, an epic enterprise.

This poem has some inspired lines, intending to carry a heavy weight of meaning that is not always clear, but Auden is patiently taking up a poetic voice here that teeters on the brink of Dylan Thomas's:

> 'And the hard bright light composes
> A meaningless moment into an eternal fact.'

yet the scheme of the whole work is to give an impressionistic account of the 'birth' of the city in the human imagination. With the added

Christian perspective of the inevitable consequences of the Fall the poem takes us into territory part-Romantic and part-baroque. It is a dialogue between Auden's two poetic selves, the builder, the maker at odds with the voice of reason, taking comfort in established culture. 'The ruins of the post-Vergilian city' lead to statements of Cassandra-like negativity:

'Henceforth division was also to be her condition'

Yet, like several twentieth century writers who expressed ambivalent feelings about the city as a human/humane community (such as D. H. Lawrence), Auden ends his historical survey with an assertion that metropolis, the 'too great city' is opposed to the 'conscious city' and he ends with a fundamental opposition to that creation as if it has been spawned by forces of Unreason:

'. . . . . . . to all who dwell on
the public side of her mirrors, resentments and no peace.'

This is one of Auden's most impassioned and successful poems, and, it could be argued, shows his true strengths as a lyric poet who constantly felt the impulse to describe rather than interpret.

Essentially, Auden sees *homo ludens*, playful man, as the creature of this cold, angular metropolis. His vision is one that delineates the human presence in that massive expression on non-place: the city. So many writers, poets and artists tell us that the city is now too large-scale to be colonised by anything at all like the 'love' Auden constantly insists on as the saviour of what is truly human in us. Recent research in Britain shows that many cities are typical of Leeds, for instance, in which only 900 people out of a population of 700,000 live in the city centre.

Auden's post-Vergilian city is closer to the Italian conception, and at this time, Auden was living in Ischia, at ease with his place and adjusted to a new perspective on his self-identity. The latter was under threat when he contemplated the metropolis as an urbane, 'baroque' social poet. With these reflections, it is relevant here to point out that Auden's writing on landscape - both historical and in terms of living space - relate to a central poetic tradition which remind Auden that a persona is needed to provide a commentary. He does so by providing the voice of exile. So often, he takes up a stance of the poet in some kind of metaphorical exile from what is truly cultural, like the Roman poet Ovid among the Goths. This idea of the urbane, 'civilised' poet being forced to live among the stock figures of rural simplicity has been a standing joke in much English poetry, as well as a genuine lament - from Shakespeare's *As You Like It* to the elegies of Peter Russell. Auden is himself aware of this ambivalence, and actually addresses the theme directly in 'Et in Arcadia Ego' where once again, the centre of the poem is a dynamic image of modernity;

'I well might think myself
A humanist.
Could I not manage to see
How the autobahn
Thwarts the landscape
In godless Roman arrogance. . . .'

so turning the cliché of the Roman poet Ovid, banished to the sleepy provinces away from the cultivated literary circles in Roma, inside out. The new barbarians are, paradoxically, the children of the city-makers, and the rural landscape of the rural literary traditions are in brutal foreground, as he tells us that the farmer's children

'Tip-toe past the shed
Where the gelding-knife is kept.'

With this short poem, it should be noted that Auden's insistence on shock, on reshuffling the familiar in literary contexts, in increasingly his stock ammunition in the 'Fifties and 'Sixties. What holds all the commentaries and speculations together is his use of history, particularly in an age when the uses of history were being revised in the light of the atomic bomb, new individual freedom and the rethinking of moral and personal education. What to do with freedom remains a preoccupation in the last phase of Auden's work. Place, landscape and allegory have been explored and used as effective vehicles for detached insights into the descent of man.

V PAST AND PRESENT

A major feature of Auden's work lies in his interest in the past - his sense of significant history: whether as a type of discourse relating identity to formative events or as a point of reference for defining ideas. A sense of history is often the basis for a typical Auden poem. Much of Auden's later work has a series of very purposeful contrasts between periods in history when barbarism and civilisation collide. But he also includes his moral interests in this. This generally means that he comments on a decline, a descent of man from some supposed peak of 'civilisation'. The psychologist Ronald Fairbairn talks of a final stage of emotional development which he calls mature dependence when 'total autonomy was both impossible and undesirable'. Auden sees some kind of similarity between the course of history as inevitable decline and the progress of our moral selves. He asserts the connection between individual and collective responsibility.

Yet history as a theme is also a part of a wide critique of the modern condition, and this is dealt with in *The Shield of Achilles*. Here, art and historical process are concurrently handled.

A statement in Auden's essay *The Poet and the City* is helpful at this point because he discusses the production of art in the modern context:

> 'It is difficult for a modern artist to believe he can make an enduring object when he has no model of endurance to go by; he is more tempted than his predecessors to abandon the search for perfection. . . .'

A great deal of the later poetry, from the 'Fifties onwards, is concerned with the inter-relationships of historical change, art and morality.

The Shield of Achilles deals with a paradox in this area of enquiry. Achilles, hero of the Trojan War described in Homer's epic *The Iliad*, represents the killing machine, the force of destruction epitomised by the strong, war-glorious male. The god of fire, Hephaestos, has made the shield, but Achilles is still doomed as he is vulnerable in spite of this magnificent armoury. Auden makes the shield a symbol of visionary intelligence, a pageant of suffering, building up to the image of war in the penultimate stanza that equal Goya's paintings and etchings of the Napoleonic War:

'That girls are raped, that two boys knife a third,
Were axioms to him, who'd never heard
Of any world where promises were kept. . . . .'

The poem takes on the problem about evil in the divinely-created world, and man's potential for inflicting misery on man. As usual with Auden, though, time goes by as normal. The human world within the machinations of history has a constant of bored normality. Lives go on just the same, caught up in momentous events:

'Barbed wire enclosed an arbitrary spot
Where bored officials lounged (one cracked a joke)
And sentries sweated for the day was hot. . .'

Clio, the muse of history in Greek mythology, makes several appearances in the 'Fifties poems, and notably as a relentless force for change, for functionality. It is a Machiavellian view of people caught up in time and its demands:

'Clio loves those who bred them better horses,
Found answers to their questions, made their things.'

In other words, Auden was taking an interest, before the arrival of the New Historicism, of history as a cultural narrative. He did not have the tools to theorise about this, but basically, his poems about history discuss, and look for, significance in history as narrative. History as narrative was the way that the subject had been taught in English schools for generations. In *Makers of History* for instance, he refers to the way that 'legend' justly 'makes into one' our images of a time or of a person. His poems about historical process lead to final questions about our knowledge of ourselves through the cultural mediation of 'history' as a subject, as a package of meanings:

'Simple to add how Greatness, incognito,
Admired plain-spoken comment on itself
By Honest John. . . . .'

Auden's clearest statement of his interest in our sense of being individual, of being fully alive within this huge perspective of history comes in *Homage to Clio*. It was Philip Larkin's review of this in 1960 that formed a negative view of Auden's later poetry. Larkin said that it was 'too verbose to be memorable and too intellectual to be moving'. There is some justification in the insistence on the intellectualism being too prominent, but equally, it could be argued that no serious attempt has been made to understand Auden's persona in much of the poetry written between c. 1955 and 1965.

One reason for this criticism has been the persistence of a touchstone of the cultured man of letters behind the lyric voice; whether or not this is Auden himself is not important. He merely puts a presence in the poems who is an extension of a type, a representative consciousness. In *The Epigoni* he is there as a 'cultured gentleman' but in *Homage to Clio* Auden moves into new territory with a lyric voice which is trying to negotiate a discourse about our sense of being alive inside the enigmatic historical process. The poem begins with an assertion that every being in creation is simply 'of itself' and that life will carry on regardless of individual suffering or joy:

'. . . . . a new generation of birds who chirp,
Not for effect, but because chirping
Is the thing to do.'

The poem stresses the sense of human isolation in the awareness of being a living organism in a huge world of sensual activity. It compares with Yeats's great lines from 'Sailing to Byzantium':

'That is no country for old men. The young
In one another's arms, birds in the trees,
Those dying generations - at their song. . . .'

but whereas Yeats is interested in the centrality of art in such thoughts of visionary immortality, Auden is happy to place art and poetry as something that simply happens, like everything else in the 'normal' world: 'To observation/ my book is dead'.

Auden is far more interested in the sheer physicality of our being in the world. His narrator is a biological function: a composite of awareness and animal acceptance. Time is a silent process that has no response; it runs like a machine:

'. . . . . Your silence already is there
Between us and any magical centre
Where things are taken in hand.'

Which leads to his affirmation we can only live if we believe we are significant - and that love and art, as part of the same impulse- are what saves us from being simply dumb chroniclers of change around us.

'No explosion can conquer but a lover's Yes
Has been known to fill. So few of the Big
Ever listen. . . .'

Where is poetry in all this - for the professional such as Auden? He debates the issues around the notion of being dedicated to the art of poetry as if it was worth no more than a bird's 'chirp'. In the scheme of time, poetry has no importance:

'I dare not ask you if you bless the poets,
For you do not look as if you ever read them,
Nor can I see a reason why you should.'

Much of Auden's poetry at this time belittles art and culture and then paradoxically places it as central to the idea of being reclaimed to humanity in a Godless age. A drifting sense of being will lead to an affirmation of the place of art and poetry in this crisis of selfhood. It is hard to see where any intellectualism clutters up this particular poem. Larkin's criticism seems to be wildly generalised. If anything, this poem seeks for a way to explain the problem of consciousness and how we try to understand being in a confusing and meaningless world, and it does this in an approachable way. It is, in fact, as passionate a statement about time and the human sense of awe and smallness as is Dylan Thomas's *Poem in October* or *Fern Hill*. Auden is trying to deal with a subject which many writers in recent years have tried to write about at much greater length. His friend Isherwood, for instance, devotes a long opening chapter of his novel *A Single Man*, written in 1963 (published in 1964) to this subject. His character George is presented as an organism, a human animal in a framework of chaotic meaninglessness. The human mind takes a back seat and the body is the centre of interest.

Much of Auden's poetry is indicative of this feeling of a loss of certainty in a world in which 'power' is detached from common humanity and operates unobserved. His poems about history are also about change, about being an individual and about hanging on to a range of values which stem from classical precepts. So many of the later poems have allusions to classical literature and to the beginnings of humanism that a critic has to deal with issues of modernity and what it means to be a citizen of the 'city'.

Power

Increasingly, Auden becomes immersed in thinking about power. In the post-second world war atmosphere, it was difficult for writers to avoid exploring themes and subjects related to massive, impersonal edifices of power. The 'Fifties and 'Sixties produced a body of serious literature that felt it had to restate the position of the individual in a frame of advancing de-humanised power in society. Auden, the American, saw this in the context of the management revolution. It was in the USA that Henry Ford's mass production techniques originated. The leader of the 'scientific' school of management, Taylor, invented work measurement and put about the idea that the worker's sole reason for being was productivity. Man was being reinvented as a mechanism. It is no accident that in these years Isaac Asimov fictionalised robotics, dystopias were written, bomb culture was confronted by new humanist values and sexual liberation was a weapon against the emerging corporate state. Anything that would subsume the individual into corporate power be anathema to Auden, the Christian poet. He insisted in believing in man's special place - his difference from other species.

Taylorism wanted to streamline business functions so that annoying concepts such as 'work satisfaction' would not confuse the aim of reaching target production figures. Corporate man was becoming part of Marshall McLuhan's idea of the extensions of man. We were being mechanised to the point at which all machines, said McLuhan, were potentially an integral part of us. The vision was bleak. Auden takes an intriguing stance on this in his poem *The Managers* and the bleakness becomes a lot more interesting-in fact it examines man who has power as the antithesis of any previous concept of the heroic or the impressive:

'The last word on how we may live or die

Rests today with such quiet

Men, working too hard in rooms that are too big.'

The managers are stealthy, unobserved; they have only one element of humanity and that is their desire for order, their backs bent 'over some report' . Their idea of power is dedication to quantifiable data, not human qualities. Auden is imagining a product of a system which has nothing to do with established relationships - he is tapping into that line of thought that resists anonymity.

If the new version of power brings with it a new, emergent human type, a functional animal, what place is there for error? The idea appealing to Auden reminds one of his abiding absorption with the abuse of power by individuals. The frightening concept behind all this is perfection. In *The History of Science* he says:

'Dare sound Authority confess
That one can err his way to riches,
Win glory by mistake, his dear
Through sheer wrong-headedness?'

That is to say, Auden is concerned by a radical redefinition of humanity as striving to attain the perfection of order, rational control and even an attempt to impose a rationality on the designed future. Again, he uses popular culture to interpret this obsession with perfection and the American social context is more relevant here than any other. One of his most successful forays into this territory is *Limbo Culture*. This takes up the notion that there is a sophistication made along with this new human formula for power and order which generates a 'love for inexactness' in the stories about itself. In the new popular culture, the narratives about ourselves convey a necessary doubt, a self-immolation in ideas and words:

'The language spoken by the tribes of Limbo
has many words far subtler than our own
To indicate how much, how little something
. . . . . Nor do its pronouns distinguish between persons'

Auden has a vision of another race, in cultural terms, inside the given, established 'other'. His lyric voice sees a distance and a difference between those like himself who live simply but fully, and those who are a hidden race, the indeterminate, uniform middle class. A whole sub-culture is voiced in the poem; a hidden, receding voice of dissent from the narrator.

Auden is somehow talking about the 'limbo' of that condition of stasis, of being caught in time unable to move to completion - an earthly purgatory. The ultimate power is self-knowledge, and these unfortunates, despite their 'success' find that it eludes them:

'............... Could it be
A limbo tribesman only loves himself?
For that, we know, cannot be done exactly'

It is possible to expand on the implications of that pronoun 'we' in this case. Auden had become in a sense a champion of the dissenting élite who wrote serious articles in *Encounter* - the journal of intellectual discourse for liberal middle class thinkers. He was the 'official voice' of the 'establishment' of poetry who had also preserved in his writing acute perceptions of weakness, of engulfing disorder. There was a considerable doubt about the place of the intellectual in Western society in these years and Auden somehow set out to prove that important things could be said and written in the face of the advancing influence of popular culture.

In 'Limbo Culture', the 'Dragon and the knight set to with fang and sword' but always 'miss their rival'. This uncertainty, the void in the centre of the seemingly assured culture of success is his target, and the pronoun 'we' is an ironic voice, where the persona in the poem accounts for a difference which is passé, irrelevant. It defends a lost certainty about what our stories tell of our social identities. Auden's question as to whether a limbo tribesman only loves himself is answered by another kind of uncertainty: the lyric voice in the poem cannot be sure of anything, except uncertainty.

Power, then, in personal and in social terms, deals again with the familiar Auden pattern of thought embedded in descriptions of a personal, small scale and domestic definition of being . But he cannot leave the thematic interest in using stories, myths and fairy tales to give the reader an ironic viewpoint on these serious concerns. The poems of this period are populated by the 'Ugly Princess' and the 'Knight'. The tension between our waking lives and the hidden subconscious narratives about time and life we all share is an easy device for Auden to use to write about something indefinable. 'There is less grief than wonder on the whole' (from *Objects*) partly sums up this attitude.

Wonder is what stays with us, inside, part of our personal landscape that forms our sense of being and purpose.

By the late 'Fifties, fresh elaborations on some of these themes were about to grow; Auden's beliefs and social commentaries were solidifying more visibly, and he was clearly looking for a way to simplify, to move to a microcosm rather than a massive scale. In the greater world, *homo ludens* could 'play' with power in 'Limbo culture' but there was always the self and his emotions to return to: the subconscious voice that will not go away. Faith can be one way of defining the way we have to live and accept compromise, keeping the wonder to the surface:

> 'Poems which make us cry direct us to
> Ourselves at our least apt. . . . .'

Meaning that we can understand some inner being who is certain of the value of our emotional lives only at times of challenge or crisis. In the ordinary, mundane world of making money and procreating, this inner self is quiescent. So much religious experience in Auden's poetry is a lament for the erasing of that inner self.

Horae Canonicae

This sequence of seven poems is based on the canonical hours of the church and they also cover the particular duties associated with each hour of the day. The poems expound the microcosmic span of diurnal existence; the first being awakening into life as if at a new birth and the last two dealing with sleep, death and isolation. The theme of our being locked into an incommunicable self takes on more detail in these poems. The physicality of biological perceptions written about in the domestic Auden (*About the House*) are here enlarged into very ambitious lines, technically full of interest and with a diction that unites a stock of language ranging from ecclesiastical terms to slang. Reading these poems demands a knowledge of the terminology of Christian thought, but the interest in the present context is mainly in the account of self-knowledge contained here.

In *Prime* for instance, the lines:

'Still the day is intact, and I
The Adam sinless in our beginning.'

is reminiscent of George Herbert, the seventeenth century priest-poet, whose *The Temple* deals with the symbolic geography of a church from porch to altar. Auden is fascinated by this kind of microcosmic geography, and he wrote a secular version in his collection *About the House* in 1966. The Metaphysical poetry of which Herbert was an exponent, is also typified by wit and wordplay, moving from the comic to the serious and using overlapping reference. Auden enjoys this and makes it part of his scheme.

To understand what he is trying to do in *Horae Canonicae*, a close study of one poem would help, and *Nones* is most relevant to the present stage in Auden's life.

Nones

Nones is in seven 16-line sections, rhymed and unrhymed lines mixed. The first section creates an impressionistic atmosphere of the scene after Christ's death on the cross. It is mid-afternoon and the course of life mirrored in the drama of the poem is one of decline, a sense of loss and error. Section Two tells of the vanished crowd of voyeurs and a reflection on Jesus' influence. Then comes an account of inaction after such trauma:

'Outliving our act, we stand where we are,
As discharged as some
Discarded artifact of our own,'

The fourth section narrates a vision of the durability of this significant death in that continuum. Following this, an image of evil in the world after such failure as Adam's - a sin they still sense. The penultimate section splits into a dual explanation of identity at this point of loss and rebirth- another self always frightens us - a conscience - after such a deed of sacrifice:

'. . . . . to a room
Lit by one weak bulb, where our double sits
Writing and does not look up.'

Nones ends with a passage focused on the possibility of reconciliation with that part of being human we deny: the truth of Christ's sacrifice - being expressed in Auden's favourite terminology - that of the ordinary, physical world of the senses 'awed by death'.

The sequence presents difficulties of syntax and of overall patterns of meaning; the end result is not always consistent or clear and the reader needs help, as for example when the terms utopian and arcadian are contrasted. But *Nones* shows the typical features of the sequence: cryptic, delphic images of a vision of two identities within us. All that remains after such an imaginative straining to picture the central, formative event of western consciousness, is simply a return to living. Stanza five is the turning back into life, and this is a key motif in Auden's poetry. Again and again, the poetic voice, the cultured persona, moves from an ordinary ecstasy back into life. Normality, in Clio's spell, makes us define ourselves by making stories and also by finding small satisfactions in the normal life we turn away to after a vision. We

'Mythify, use this event
While, under a hotel bed, in prison,
Down wrong turnings, its meaning
Waits for our lives.'

Clearly, there is more guilt here than anything else, as with so many religious poems, and the doubts we have as critics about any visionary attempts to deal with historical moments are always there. We are asked to envisage the grand and the awesome. Again, Auden borrows from Dylan Thomas and the Metaphysical Poets in order to achieve this, and it is typical of him that such diverse references should be there. The depth of allusion can sometimes be as formidable with Auden as it is with T. S. Eliot.

About the House

These poems are 'a cycle about what worldliness really means' and the idea behind them is to investigate and celebrate a living space: to develop what was noted earlier as Auden's abiding interest in the physicality, the sense of being in the world as a functioning organism with a space to live in. The specific house in mind is his home in Kirchstetten, Austria, and it is useful to recall here that he had had many happy years in houses in Ischia, in the U. S. A and in England. But Kirchstetten had become a bolthole, a nest, a workspace.

The focal interest in these poems lies in what is said about creativity and the life of an artist. *The Cave of Making* - the study - is a poem addressed to Louis MacNeice, with whom he had travelled to Iceland in the 'Thirties. What is given here as a profile of a creative habit and about the nature of poetry, is central to an understanding of Auden's poetry, particularly in later life. The lines that hint at a deep preoccupation are:

> 'Who would, for preference,
>
> Be a bard in an oral culture
>
> Obliged at drunken feasts to improvise a eulogy
>
> Of some beefy illiterate burner. . . . .'

and here is a paradox that invites a criticism of Auden which is easy to express. His conception of poetry is clearly that it lies unsteadily between the entertaining light verse he defended so well and the poetry of the *vates,* the professional maker of images who invests a literate culture with a voice of moderation, tolerance and philosophic reflection. The paradox is that a bard , though potentially sophisticated, need not necessarily be a slave to a 'cave of making' which demands total dedication. The poet can live openly among the audience,be a tradesman in words as well as a professional elsewhere. In other words, the exclusivity, the special status of the life of art is the principal idea here. In his prose meditations, *Dichtung und Wahrheit* (truth and design) he had discussed some of these things, and the German words, taken from Goethe, reflect the insoluble problem of trying to reconcile the uncertainties of life with the designs and forms of art, just as Auden had pointed out about the two Housman's in his 'Thirties review.

Thus, from his youth, Auden saw poetry as a vocation with a special place in cultural constructions. Poetry must connect with people - with friendship and must express the fullness of human feelings which are integral to the personality.

For this reason, *About the House* is arguably the most relaxed, natural Auden voice. What he calls 'the Country of Unconcern' around the poet's 'cave' is very likely the world as discussed in the most celebrated metaphorical cave in literature: Plato's cave of illusion in *The Republic*. In this cave, the inhabitants in the darkness of their cave have a fire, and in the flickering firelight they only ever see the passers-by in shadow, never seeing real people at first-hand. The person who could come to them and talk to them of the reality would be in the uneasy situation of artist-liar-madman. Auden's metaphorical cave is an oblique reference to this. It is the role of the poet and the man he is part of, to speak the truth, whatever.

Friendship is pivotal to all this. The rooms of the house, the physical arena for eating, drinking, making love as well as for writing poetry, are significant to Auden's notions of belonging, in every sense. For instance, a poem about the toilet, *The geography of the House* is dedicated to Isherwood, one of his oldest friends, and the joke is hard to miss. The poem wittily develops the importance of understanding the mind-body differences in the way we cope with our understanding nature. 'Mind and body run on different timetables' and our 'morning visit' leaves the dead concerns of yesterday behind. He has found symbolism and patterns of meaning even in defecation.

Poem IX, *For Friends Only* crystallises the theme of friendship very neatly:

'Easy at first, the language of friendship
Is, as we soon discover,
Very difficult to speak well. . . .'

and the poem celebrates the welcoming, entertaining function of a house. 'You are unlikely to encounter dragons or romance' here, but normality and habit are assured. It will be a place to talk easily, exchange ideas and so on. The developing mood of the sequence is increasingly one of a mix of bohemian indulgence and spiritual ease. The classic Roman belief in the gods of the home, the lares and penates, is a foundation of the poems' cultural reference. Friendship is always hand-in-hand with the ideals of the Roman 'Good life' of *simplicitas* and *felicitas*.

Auden saw the significance of the idea of a home in its fullest sense. Theodore Zeldin, in his *Intimate History of Humanity* has expressed this well:

(Home is. . .) where one both takes care of others and is taken care of, while also having the right to be left alone, and if it is one of the great collective and personal works of art that all humans spend their lives attempting to raise up. . . it still remains within the province of magic. . . .'

Zeldin expresses succinctly what Auden is intrigued by: the properties of domesticity to effect transformations and create fresh layers of identity: renewal derived from both security and space for thought and objective reflection. When Auden imagined his Eden in 'Vespers' he said 'in my Eden each observes his compulsive rituals and superstitious tabus but we have no morals. . .' and there seems to be some tenuous link in his poetry between asserting friendship and stating the tenets of faith. Love and home are twins towers of the city of contentment.

VI CONCLUSIONS

In his later poetry, Auden brings together several of the preoccupations established in the early poetry, but the persistent focus is in the expanding and maturing definition of love. Auden's poems about power and politics are never quite as assured and successful as the poems which deal with the personal life. In his daydream college for bards, in his essay *The Poet and the City* he insists that 'Every student would be required to look after a domestic animal and cultivate a garden plot.' There is in this comfortable, avuncular tone too much that has been called Audenesque, but the smile from time to time reveals bare teeth at times, and there is an anger at man's inhumanity to man.

'Love is substantial. All luck is good' - a line from one of his last poems - not only encapsulates Auden's view on the experience of the random, enigmatic life we have to cope with, but also his poetic voice. His poetry has a quality of marketplace oracle. You could go to him for spiritual advice but he would offer intellectual games rather than meditation or prayer.

The mature emotional stage referred to earlier may have been, in the end, anathema to a poet such as Auden. Humour is always there, black or carefree; academic courses and examinations largely ignore this element, but it is at the heart of his approach to writing.

This study began with an attempt to define an Auden poem, and it now seems fitting to end with a judgement on his later poetry, a body of work which has been much denigrated. Ian Sansom, in an essay summarising Auden's poetic reputation, says:

> 'The standard view, then, was that Auden was finished: his work unserious, his reputation declining. According to John Fletcher, writing in The Spectator, "Auden, who has known vogue in the past, seems to be a rather unfashionable poet these days"'

and Sansom rightly points out that a younger generation have taken him up. Why? I think that one answer can be found in a contrast of two of his last poems. The first, *Loneliness* openly voices his need for

Chester Kallman and how he is missed. It is entirely honest and as direct as a thunderbolt hitting a tree. The second, *The Horatians*, is a stoical mix of wit and wry admission of a negative impulse about his generation of intellectuals and writers. *Loneliness* demonstrates what he can achieve when he removes the veil of the intellect, the thinking machine in Auden the poet which insists on finding tropes, demonstrative illustrations, cross-currents and allusions to enrich his subject. The poem is a simple meditation on loss, with a severe Augustan diction balanced and sometimes effaced by slangy frankness:

'History counsels patience,
tyrants come, like plagues, but none
can rule the roost for ever.'

juxtaposed with 'tomorrow/ Chester, my chum, will return.' The poem is intensely passionate, about the struggle to carry on in isolation, the automatic self which writes a letter and cats is somehow separated from the self that grieves, laments. Auden is writing directly, and effectively about that dichotomy.

Classical and literary allusions may assure him of the functions of the bard in an 'oral culture', but that oral culture needs now, more than ever, to find in poetry something redemptive of human feelings. Auden is tacitly asserting that there were less hectic, changeable times in which poetry was a small-scale art, with a monopoly on communication of important thoughts by the 'important' for the 'important'.

Auden is acutely aware of all this in his later poems. Critics have not pinpointed this nor credited it sufficiently, concentrating instead on easy, rather fastidious carping about occasional or indulgent poems. *The Horatians* addresses these questions of the poet's place in a society which is engendering a new-revisionist - definition of culture as an entertainment or diversion from time's certainty. The parallels with the Roman amphitheatre in Horace's time do not escape Auden. The Horatians in the time of the greatest Latin poets were indeed lamenting the grossness around them, but also coming to terms with a new barbarity which would somehow be absorbed because that was

71

the way of the world. Auden's conclusions about the 'Horatians' of his own time, were accepting, understanding.

'. . . . . We can only
do what it seems to us we were made for,
look at this world with a happy eye
but from a sober perspective.'

Philip Larkin criticises this Horatian element as 'Hollywood Lempriere' (referring to the famous classical dictionary) as if Auden is somehow using his classical education to show off, to convey a *gravitas* to a narcissistic society in need of a sober sage. In some ways, Auden did self-consciously play the part of sage and grand old man of letters, but the point that Larkin misses is that all this allusion was integral to Auden's vision of the way the world was going and with what crass priorities. He never succumbed to nostalgia, but used constructions of the past to bring them to bear on the crisis of the present.

Some of the later poems jar the sensibility; this is partly because Auden is guilty about his homosexuality, and also defiant. In this defiance one finds the source of that buoyancy and sheer pleasure in living with others that one finds also in Isherwood's fiction. Although some poems border on the banal, and he never edited or revised with a detachment that would have avoided doggerel, there is usually something of merit in a stanza or a couplet. But this is not a defence of sloppiness - simply an excuse for second-best work which never really seems admissible.

There were many other Audens, too. He anthologised with affection and enthusiasm. His taste for humorous, light verse led to an injection of whimsicality in a serious poetry world and reminded readers that poetry written for the page is not necessarily an essential monopoly, as poetry and song were once only one art.

The question of his influence on other poets is difficult to assess with any certainty, but there is a definite sense that the poetry of Heaney and others who have taken the art as a serious vocation owe him a debt. Several poets now write with things to say about the way we live now as well as giving a vision of the future, and in a discourse that is not afraid of convention. Auden's contemporary diction has been a force for renewal too - in a different sense from that of Larkin and The Movement. Auden's words are playfully explosive mixtures of academic and slangy, American demotic and playroom banal. Younger poets have been able to take similar formulae for innovation with a feeling of permission, as Auden himself had shown the way.

VII CRITICAL APPROACHES: NOTES FOR STUDENTS

As Auden's work makes such demands on the student, and this guide has been necessarily brief and selective (The Collected Poems run to about 900 pages) it may be helpful here to suggest some broad approaches to the poetry, most of them tried and tested - and familiar. The basic split is between the stance that sees the social Auden - the commentator, and the psychoanalytical approach.

There has certainly been a dissentient voice as well, as the decades after his death have brought about revisions in the perceived social purpose of poetry, and it is easy to see an élitist assumption in much of the material forming the basis of his art. Therefore, some perspectives offer a negative view, albeit well-meaning and done in the service of truth.

Dissent and satire

It is tempting to find in both concepts Auden the Christian and Auden the 'Thirties youth a voice of dissent. There was a great deal to be unhappy about in the representations of authority and power in these contexts. Superficially, the Auden of the anthologies appears as exactly this type of poet. *The Unknown Citizen*, for instance, is extremely popular in schools anthologies but hardly represents the norm. But it is profitable for a critic to ask what Auden laments in *The Age of Anxiety* and why he repeatedly returns to the use of classical literature and history as some kind of safe criterion, some indistinct Augustan touchstone of cultured safety for his bargainings about a better and fuller life. the age of Augustus in Rome was the great age of satire, as was the Augustan age in English literature, encompassing Dryden, Swift and Pope, but Auden never fully accepts the moral stance, so this line of thought is always fraught with problems.

However, there are few more exciting texts to work on if one wants to discover the issues around popular as opposed to classical, book-based cultural assumptions and interests. Auden does make one look up sources and go outside his poems for a depth of enquiry. When one reads *Musée des Beaux Arts* there is a need to check out Breughel's painting of Icarus or the poem does not work at all.

Whether Auden is a satirist in the sense that he always looks for an interpretation of folly and the abuse of human qualities or powers is debatable; in comparison with, say Orwell, he is slight and impressionistic. There is no world-view, just a series of doubts. No pattern seems to be shaped. But if one accepts that Auden's contribution to satire is typified in the epistle, then *Letter to Lord Byron* has few equals in sheer exuberance and delight in rhyming and word-play.

In the end, his self-undermining lyric personae leads to satire, and his poetry highlights the ills of a given culture by focusing on an individual, much as a stand-up comedian might do. The only caveat here is that the question has to be asked: what segment of society did Auden represent in his last two decades? If he did represent at all, one has to say it is the voice of alienated élitist intellectuals increasingly unsure of their place in what is increasingly a culture led, and saturated with, popular tastes - 'post-modernism'. This term includes the notion that art and media forms will draw references, allusions and quotations from any other form at random, and it is an irony that his allusive method was one which tried to put shape and sense into such practices.

Psychoanalytic approaches

Auden valued psychoanalysis. His interest in Freud's work on the unconscious is perceptible in all periods of his writing. His symbolic use of figures from folktales reminds one of the fundamental works on how writing can enlighten the narratives we create inside ourselves, Bruno Bettelheim's *The Uses of Enchantment*. Here, Bettelheim looks at the importance of fairy tales and stories read to us in childhood, and how these persist, transform and lead into self-concepts and even conditions of phobia and lack of conviction about being in the world.

The diction from such narratives pepper Auden's work. The nanny, the dragon, the mother, the witch, the forest and so on. The world of Grimm and Anderson is never far away, and this adds an uncanny and idiosyncratic element to the serious verse commentaries he offers.

But in recent years, with the growth of critical theory as a way of adding new dimensions to critical assessments of texts, this approach has been opened up in more interesting ways. Texts such as Conrad's *Heart of Darkness*, a 'voyage to the interior' narrative, has been extended and interpreted as a subconscious, symbolic story growing from Conrad's own inner dimensions and uncertainties. Auden's autobiographical poems lend themselves to this form of analysis, particularly *About the House* and *The Age of Anxiety*. Auden's Christian faith deepens and complicates the issue, but the psycho-analytic approach repays the effort put into it.

Love and our time

Few readers can be unaware that Auden championed the centrality of emotions of love as a redeeming, regenerative force on our sense of ourselves. His statement 'We must love one another or die' has entered the world of postcards and media reproductions. The critical approach is to see his writing about love as touching on three areas:
- the love which is *caritas* - love for all humanity;
- the love for another human being which repeats Christ's love as he taught it;
- and our care for creation, our regard for all life.

In the simplest, short lyrics of imaginative empathy for others, such as *Roman Wall Blues*, he asks us to see history as people, as feeling, and that the emotions called love are something which embrace and supercede all other needs and aspirations. Despite his mistrust of romantic love, he offers plenty of other options.

As a gay writer, he also has another dimension to offer to constructions of the 'norms' in our culture, just as we find, for instance, with E. M. Forster's character of Aziz in *A Passage to India* where we have to try to understand a type of maleness, a sort of androgyny of the spirit which infuses the language. There is much critical work still to be done on Auden considered as a gay writer.

Any critical approach to his poetry with this objective must be aware of the shifting meanings and nuances given to the word love. However, one constant application is in terms of the need for another to bring about a completeness of identity:

'With love's fidelity and love's weakness.'

and here we have a hint as to how a critical assessment of such an elusive subject must take account of an immense amount of biographical material, despite the theoretical notions of the New Criticism which insist that we should treat a poem as a linguistic artefact. Auden would have enjoyed the speculations of some critics into Freudian dynamics in very honest, confessional texts where the writer simply wants to examine a phase of life or an isolated incident, with no hidden depths which need an 'expert' to unravel meanings.

SELECT BIBLIOGRAPHY

(a) Works by Auden

Collected Poems edited by Edward Mendelson (London, Faber 1976)

The English Auden edited by Edward Mendelson (London, Faber 1977)

The Dyer's Hand (London, Faber 1962)

A Certain World (London, Faber 1971)

Forewords and Afterwords (London, Faber 1973)

with Louis Macneice *Letters from Iceland* (London, Faber 1937)

with Christopher Isherwood *The Dog Beneath the Skin* (London, Faber 1935)

Journey to a War (London, Faber 1948)

The Ascent of F6 and *On the Frontier* (London, Faber 1948)

(b) Biography

Carpenter, Humphrey *W. H. Auden* (London, OUP 1992)

Davenport-Hines, Richard *Auden* (London, Heinemann 1995)

Osborne, Charles *W. H. Auden* (London, Methuen 1979)

Smith, Stan *W. H. Auden* (London, OUP 1985)

Spender, Stephen *World within World* (London, Hamish Hamilton 1951)

Spender, Stephen *W. H. Auden: A Tribute* (London, Weidenfeld 1974)

(c) Works on Auden

Buell, Frederick *W. H. Auden as a Social Poet* (Ithaca and London, 1973)

Duchene, Francois *The Case of the Helmeted Airman* (London, Chatto 1972)

Haffenden, John (editor) *W. H. Auden: The Critical Heritage* (London, Routledge 1983)

Hoggart, Richard *W. H. Auden* (London, Longman's 1957)

Hoggart, Richard *'The Long Walk - The Poetry of W. H. Auden'* in Speaking to Eachother Vol. 2 About Literature (London, Penguin 1970) pp. 53-88

Hynes, Samuel *The Auden Generation: Literature and Politics in the Thirties* (London Bodley Head 1976)

Isherwood, Christopher *'Some Notes on Auden's Early Poetry'* in Exhumations (London, Penguin 1969) pp. 29-34

Larkin, Philip *'What became of Wystan?'* in Required Writing (London, Faber 1983) pp. 123-8

Melchiori, Giorgio *The Tightrope Walkers* (Greenwood Press, Westport, Connecticut, 1974)

Reeves, James *The Poets and their Critics* (London, Hutchinson 1969)

Spears, Monroe K, *Auden: A Collection of Critical Essays* (New Jersey, Prentice Hall 1964)

Whitehead, John *'Auden: an early poetical notebook'* in London Magazine NS no. 2 May 1965 pp. 85-93

(d) Literary background and wider studies

Bergonzi, Bernard *Reading the Thirties:Texts and Contexts* (London, Macmillan 1978)

Cunningham, Valentine *British Writers of the Thirties* (London, OUP 1989)

Fraser, G. S. *The Modern Writer and his World* (London, Deutsch 1953 rev. 1964)

Kettle, Arnold *'W. H. Auden: Poetry and Politics in the 30's* in Clark, John et alia, *Culture and crisis in Britain in the Thirties* (London, Lawrence and Wishart 1979) pp. 83-102

Kiernan, V. G. *Poets, Politics and People* (London, Verso 1989)

Leavis, F. R. *New Bearings in English Poetry* (London, Chatto 1932 new ed. 1950)

Lucas, John (editor) *The 1930's A Challenge to Orthodoxy* (London, Harvester 1978)

Maxwell, D. E. S. *Poets of the Thirties* (London, Routledge 1969)

Orwell, George *Inside the Whale and other essays* (London, Penguin 1957)

Page, Norman *The Thirties in Britain* (London, Macmillan 1990)

Press, John *A Map of Modern English Verse* (London and New York, OUP 1969)

Paulin, Tom *'Letters from Iceland: Going North'* in Lucas (ed.) see above pp. 59-77

Sisson C. H. *English Poetry 1900-1950, An Assessment* (London, Hart-Davis 1971)

Skelton, Robin *Poetry of the Thirties* (London, Penguin 1964)

Stewart, J. I. M. *Eight Modern Writers* (London, OUP 1963)

Symons, Julian *The Thirties: A Dream Revolved* (London, Faber 1975)

Thwaite, Anthony *Poetry Today 1960-1973* (London, Longman 1973)

Wilson, Edmund *The Thirties* (London, Macmillan 1980)

(e) Bibliography

Bloomfield, B. C. and Mendelson, Edward *W. H. Auden: A Bibliography 1924-69* (University of Virginia, Charlottesville 1972) 2nd. ed.

NOTES

NOTES

GREENWICH EXCHANGE BOOKS

Student Guides

Greenwich Exchange Student Guides are critical studies of major or contemporary serious writers in English and selected European languages. The series is for the Student, the Teacher and the 'common reader' and are ideal resources for libraries. *The Times Educational Supplement (TES)* praised these books saying "The style of these guides has a pressure of meaning behind it. Students should learn from that . . . . If art is about selection, perception and taste, then this is it."

(Please note that ISBN prefix 1-871551- applies)
The series includes:

W. H. Auden by Stephen Wade (-36-6)
William Blake by Peter Davies (-27-7)
The Bröntes by Peter Davies (-24-2)
Joseph Conrad by Martin Seymour-Smith (-18-8)
William Cowper by Michael Thorn (-25-0)
Charles Dickens by Robert Giddings (-26-9)
John Donne by Sean Haldane (-23-4)
Thomas Hardy by Sean Haldane (-33-1)
Seamus Heaney by Michael Thorn (-37-8)
Philip Larkin by Warren Hope (-35-8)
Shakespeare's Poetry by Martin Seymour-Smith (-22-6)
Tobias Smollett by Robert Giddings (-21-8)
Alfred Lord Tennyson by Michael Thorn (-20-X)
W.B. Yeats by Warren Hope (-34-X)

other titles planned include:
20th Century: T.S. Eliot; Ford Madox Ford; Robert Graves; Dylan Thomas
19th Century: Arnold; Jane Austen; Browning; Byron; John Clare; S.T. Coleridge; George Eliot; John Keats; Oscar Wilde; Wordsworth
18th Century: Fielding, Dr. Johnson; Alexander Pope; Richardson; Laurence Sterne; Sheridan; Dean Swift
17th Century: Congreve; Dryden; Ben Jonson; Marlowe; Milton; Rochester
Early writings: Chaucer; Skelton

European Languages
Fifty European Novels by Martin Seymour-Smith (-49-8)

French Authors:
Balzac by Wendy Mercer (-48-X)

Other titles planned include:
Apollinaire; Céline; Gide; Proust; Rimbaud; Tournier; Verlaine; Zola

German Authors:
Goethe; Heine; Thomas Mann; Rilke

OTHER GREENWICH EXCHANGE BOOKS

All paperbacks unless otherwise stated.

LITERATURE & BIOGRAPHY

"The Author, the Book & the Reader" *by Robert Giddings*
This collection of Essays analyses the effects of changing technology and the attendant commercial pressures on literary styles and subject matter. Authors covered include Dickens; Smollett; Mark Twain; Dr Johnson; John Le Carré.
ISBN 1-871551-01-0 Size A5 approx; 220pp; illus.

"In Pursuit of Lewis Carroll" *by Raphael Shaberman*
Sherlock Holmes and the author uncover new evidence in their investigations into the mysterious life and writing of Lewis Carroll. They examine published works by Carroll that have been overlooked by previous commentators. A newly discovered poem, almost certainly by Carroll, is published here. Amongst many aspects of Carroll's highly complex personality, this book explores his relationship with his parents, numerous child friends, and the formidable Mrs Liddell, mother of the immortal Alice.
ISBN 1-871551-13-7 Size 70% A4; 130pp; illus.

"Norman Cameron" *by Warren Hope*
Cameron's poetry was admired by Auden; celebrated by Dylan Thomas; valued by Robert Graves. He was described by Martin Seymour-Smith as one of ". . . the most rewarding and pure poets of his generation . . ." is at last given a full length biography. This eminently sociable man, who had periods of darkness and despair, wrote little poetry by comparison with others of his time, but always of a high and consistent quality - imaginative and profound.
ISBN 1-871551-05-6 A5 size; 250pp; illus.

"The Essential Baudelaire" *by Professor F.W. Leakey*
A chronological survey of Baudelaire's writings this book will offer for the first time in Baudelaire studies, a comprehensive survey of his writings in their full chronological development. Baudelaire's development is explored under five headings: the Verse Poet; the Novelist in Miniature; the prose Poet; the Critic and Aesthetician; the Moralist; the translator. This book will interest Baudelaire specialists as well as the general reader.
ISBN 1-871551-3 A5 size; 300pp; illus.

PHILOSOPHY

"Marx: Justice and Dialectic" *by James Daly*
Department of Scholastic Philosophy, Queens University, Belfast.
James Daly shows the humane basis of Marx's thinking, rather than the imposed "economic materialistic" views of many modern commentators. In particular he refutes the notion that for Marx, justice relates simply to the state of development of society at a particular time. Marx's views about justice and human relationships belong to the continuing traditions of moral thought in Europe.
ISBN 1-871551-28-5 A5 size; 180 pp

"Whitehead's Philosophy" *by Dr T.E. Burke*
Department of Philosophy, University of Reading
Dr. Burke explores the main achievements of this philosopher, better known in the U.S. than Britain. Whitehead, often remembered as Russell's tutor and collaborator on *Principia Mathematica*, was one of the few who had a grasp of relativity and its possible implications. His philosophical writings reflect his profound knowledge of mathematics and science. He was responsible for initiating process theology.
ISBN 1-871551-29-3 A5 size; 180pp

POETRY

"Wilderness" *by Martin Seymour-Smith*

This Seymour-Smith's first publication of his poetry for more than 20 years. This collection of 36 poems is a fearless account of an inner life of love, frustration, guilt, laughter and the celebration of others. Best known to the general public as the author of the controversial and best selling *Hardy* (1994).

ISBN 1-871551-08-0 A5 size; 64pp

Baudelaire: "Les Fleurs du Mal in English Verse"
translated by Professor F.W. Leakey

Selected poems from *Les Fleurs du Mal* are translated with parallel French texts, are designed to be read with pleasure by readers who have no French, as well as those practised in the French language.

F.W. Leakey is Emeritus Professor of French in the University of London. As a scholar, critic and teacher he has specialised in the work of Baudelaire for 50 years. He has published a number of books on Baudelaire.

ISBN 1-871551-10-2 A5 size 140pp

"Road To Autumn" *by Michael Cullup*

This is Michael Cullup's second major collection of poems after *Reading Geographies*. These poems explore the rites of passage as a man grows older, manifesting the desire to reflect on an earlier self.

ISBN 1-871551-90-9 A5 size; 80pp

"Shakespeare's Sonnets"
edited by Martin Seymour-Smith

This scholarly edition follows the original text of the 1609 Quarto - which, with newly revised notes and introduction by Seymour-Smith - provides an insight with which to judge Shakespeare's artistic intentions.

ISBN 1-871551-38-2 A5 size; 120pp

THEATRE

"Music Hall Warriors: A history of the Variety Artistes Federation" *by Peter Honri*

This is an unique and fascinating history of how vaudeville artistes formed the first effective actor's trade union in 1906 and then battled with the powerful owners of music halls to obtain fairer contracts. The story continues with the VAF dealing with performing rights, radio, and the advent of television. Peter Honri is the fourth generation of a vaudeville family. The book has a foreword by the Right Honourable John Major MP when he was Prime Minister - his father was a founder member of the VAF.

ISBN 1-871551-06-4 140pp; A4 size; illus.